THE ANATOMY OF
THE NOVEL

The Golden Bowl   1909
H. James

Other books by Marjorie Boulton

The Anatomy of Poetry
The Anatomy of Prose
The Anatomy of Drama
The Anatomy of Language

THE ANATOMY OF
THE NOVEL

MARJORIE BOULTON
M.A., B.Litt.

ROUTLEDGE & KEGAN PAUL
London, Boston and Henley

First published in 1975
by Routledge & Kegan Paul Ltd
39 Store Street,
London WC1E 7DD,
Broadway. House, Newtown Road
Henley-on-Thames
Oxon RG9 1EN and
9 Park Street,
Boston, Mass. 02108, USA
Reprinted in 1979
Set in Monotype Bembo
and printed in Great Britain by
Whitstable Litho Ltd
Whitstable, Kent

ISBN 0 7100 8135 9 (C)
ISBN 0 7100 8136 7 (P)

For

CONSTANCE ANNE MORETON
who could have read more novels
if she had not given so much
of her life to caring for
other people

with love

CONTENTS

INTRODUCTION

This small book makes no claim to be more than an elementary and popular introduction to the study of the novel; but, though for such a purpose some simplifications are inevitable, I hope they are sensible and that the reader who explores further will not have much to unlearn. To experts it should all seem obvious; but I know from years of teaching and examining that it will be less obvious to the inexperienced students for whom I have written it.

The theory of the novel came of age very late in literary studies, within no more than the last four or five decades, just as the novel itself came of age very late in the history of literature. Thus not only schoolchildren working on prescribed books, or students starting literature courses, but many busy teachers, may have some use for a simple guidebook. I do not presume to tell anyone where to go, still less to identify some single strait gate; much better critics than I have still no ultimate authority to do that; my purpose is to describe some starting-points and directions that are reasonably useful. I have tried to show how the art of the novel is, like all major arts, multiform as well as complex, and to encourage the breadth of appreciation in which I believe genuine discriminating judgment, in contrast to literary sectarianism, takes root.

I believe too that genuine literary study, though a strenuous discipline, though sometimes demanding periods of difficult and even tedious effort, has its real roots in enjoyment; so I hope that this book will help some readers, not only to read novels rather more discerningly and to discuss them more profitably, but also to relish the reading more.

Introduction

Let me record my warm thanks for helpful information or ideas from William and Meta Auld, Douglas Gregor, Dr Kathleen Hall, Kenzo Hotta; and for patient and courteous assistance from members of the staff of the Bodleian Library, the English Faculty Library, Oxford, and the Horace Barks Reference Library, Stoke-on-Trent. I am especially grateful to Dr Kathleen Hall for her substantial and admirable help in compiling the index.

My quotations from material still in copyright are all brief; but with regard to the quotations from *The Secret Agent*, *Nostromo* and *Lord Jim* an acknowledgment to J. M. Dent and Sons, Ltd and the Trustees of the Joseph Conrad Estate allows me to thank them for their patience and courtesy at earlier stages of the preparation of this book.

M.B.

THE CONCEPT OF FICTION

'with a tale which holdeth children from play, and old men from the chimney corner.'

Sir Philip Sidney: *An Apologie for Poetrie*

The novel is a branch of fiction that developed late in history; but a relish for stories seems to be as old as recorded humanity.

We love stories mostly for two reasons: our readiness to comfort and entertain ourselves with fantasy, and our curiosity and desire for insight about reality. Though these seem like opposites, it is not always easy to separate them completely.

Children pretend, perhaps noisily, to be soldiers, cowboys, nurses, animals, parents; but most adults have some fantasy life too—or audiences could not have screamed with laughter at the film made from James Thurber's wonderful story, 'The Secret Life of Walter Mitty'. Placing ourselves in fictions in which our part is gratifying is for most of us our most unrestricted freedom. We are usually very shy about our fantasies, even ashamed; we know many of them are ridiculous, often ignoble, always selfish; but fantasy is not useless. It is a cheap, accessible pleasure and an emotional safety-valve; unlike many outlets, such as a blaze of temper or act of vandalism, it harms no one else; we may waste time daydreaming, but then we can waste too much time on any amusement; sometimes, when we observe our own fantasies, they may even teach us something about our real wishes, weaknesses and intentions. Our fantasies are harmful chiefly when we confuse them with reality: daydreaming may lead us to expect too much of other people, deceive ourselves about our own motives, expect problems to solve themselves, or feel grievances against the normal difficulties of life and imperfections of others.

Great novelists have often touched upon the danger of self-deceiving fantasy: it is a favourite theme of George Eliot:

> Some day she will be able to wear any ear-rings she likes, and already she lives in an invisible world of brilliant costumes, shimmering gauze, soft satin and velvet, such as the lady's maid at the Chase has shown her in Miss Lydia's wardrobe. She feels the bracelets on her arms, and treads on a soft carpet in front of a tall mirror. (*Adam Bede*)

This is part of poor foolish Hetty Sorrel's dreams of a gentleman's love and a wealthy home: they bring her to shattering disappointment, disgrace and a sentence of transportation. In *Daniel Deronda*, Gwendolen Harleth dreams how marriage will solve her money problems, but ignores its real demands; her suitor, Grandcourt, has harsher fantasies about breaking a spirited girl; their unrealities combine to create the reality of a wretched marriage. Jane Austen often handled the dangers of fantasy enlighteningly; we can consider, for instance, Marianne in *Sense and Sensibility*. A lesser novelist who at her best wrote brilliantly on the deceptions of fantasy and the resulting disappointments is Mrs Margaret Oliphant, in for instance *Miss Marjoribanks* or *The Cuckoo in the Nest*. Probably the most famous novel stressing this theme is Flaubert's *Madame Bovary*; but most great novels include some element of how people are educated by life out of fantasy towards a better grasp of reality.

Novelists have given less attention to the aspect of fantasy as recognized self-indulgence and comforting self-entertainment; one early example is the set of imaginative drawings Jane Eyre shows to Mr Rochester. In this century some novelists, perhaps influenced by the insights of psychoanalysis, have treated the theme more fully. A well known example is Alan Sillitoe's account of the consolation of fantasy in routine factory work, in his *Saturday Night and Sunday Morning*. Denton Welch wonderfully captures a schoolboy's imaginings:

> He saw himself refusing to go to school and disappearing completely. He was alone in a small London room with a gas-ring. He was working on something at a desk. It might have been a book, or a painting, or even a wool mat. It didn't matter; it was real work, all alone, full of joy. And afterwards—lazy times cooking on the gas-ring, scraping long ringlets of chocolate into the saucepan of hot milk, tossing the omelets into the air to turn them over; or was it only pancakes that were tossed in the air?
>
> All around the room his family and the school authorities were prowling like wild beasts. They had long teeth and claws like the mad Nebuchadnezzar; but they were powerless; for the door had double Yale padlocks and four bolts, and the windows bullet-proof glass.
>
> He went out only at night, and then he climbed on to the roof of the building, where there was a contrivance rather like those aerial devices which waft money to the pay-desk in the old-fashioned drapery shops. He had only to hang on to this wire and wish, when he would find himself swishing through the air to his destination. The long-clawed, long-toothed relations and school authorities looked up and cursed as they saw him flying gloriously free a hundred feet above their heads. (*In Youth is Pleasure*)

James Joyce's *Ulysses* and many experimental novels depend much on our recognition of fantasy as part of our inner life.

Our very private habit of self-entertaining fantasy is one of

3

the springs of artistic fiction. Good friends may console and amuse one another by shared fantasies, which need more coherence and sequence than private ones: the novelist creates fantasies for a bigger audience.

Because fiction tells of things that did not happen, and fantasy can mislead us, some moralists have seen evil in all fiction. Plato rejected poets from his ideal republic; the theatres were closed during the Commonwealth puritan régime in Britain; a Quaker, Arthur J. Naish, wrote in 1862, 'Indiscriminate novel-reading, or even frequent novel-reading, is about the most dangerous employment that can occupy a young person.'[1] He admitted that a Christian might sometimes read a good novel, perhaps by Scott or Fenimore Cooper, for its educational value; but in Edmund Gosse's Calvinist home no fiction at all was allowed and his own liking for inventing stories was condemned as sinful.[2] Jane Austen's pompous and hypocritical clergyman, Mr Collins, 'protested that he never read novels'. (If he had, he might have been more sensitive to the feelings of others.)

Yet most people know the difference between a *lie* and a *fiction*. A lie is meant to deceive; a fiction is meant to entertain.

I say of Tristram Trueman, a faithful husband with a gentle, sensible wife: 'Trueman is carrying on with that fast blonde in the chemist's; you mark my words, his wife will be on to it soon, and then we shall see the fur fly. Terrible temper she has—throws plates when she doesn't get her own way.'

This is a lie, wicked and cruel; it may be believed, and if it is it will do much harm. But perhaps I just say of his bald head: 'Heard the latest? The Bluebottles' and Clothes-moths' Sporting Syndicate has taken out a lease on Tristram's head. They're going to make it into a ski run, with a honey and ragburger stall on his left ear and a chute for the kids down his nose.'

Not very polite; but this is not merely a harmless, as opposed to a vicious, lie; it is not a lie at all; no one is going to

4

believe it; it is meant as an entertaining fiction. We are not so silly as to take any novel as literally true; we are far more likely to be deceived by our own private fantasies, which spring from our own inner conflicts and wishes.

We are drawn to fiction not only by the fun of fantasy, but by our interest in reality. Even our dreams can sometimes throw some light on our emotions; people realized this long before psychoanalysis; artistic fictions are more conscious, controlled and objective than dreams. What Shelley contended of poetry is equally true of the novel:

> A man, to be greatly good, must imagine intensely and comprehensively; he must put himself in the place of another and of many others; the pains and pleasures of his species must become his own. The great instrument of moral good is the imagination; and poetry administers to the effect by acting upon the cause. (*A Defence of Poetry*, 1821)

A good novel is *true* in the sense that it gives a sincere, well observed, enlightening picture of a portion of human life. George Eliot's *Middlemarch*, Jane Austen's *Mansfield Park*, Henry Fielding's *Tom Jones*, Henry James's *Portrait of a Lady*, Joseph Conrad's *Lord Jim*, William Golding's *Lord of the Flies*, Graham Greene's *The Heart of the Matter*, tell us far more about realities of human experience than would seven evenings of 'truthful' but superficial chatter. Good fictional pictures of life widen our sympathies, help our sense of proportion, educate our moral judgment; they make human goodness, frailty, sufferings, needs, relationships far more real than abstract definitions or vague exhortations can. They may teach us more of consequences—an important part of learning to make wise decisions—for they show how character traits cause actions, and whither these lead. We may learn more about our selfishness and self-deceiving from Jane Austen, George Eliot, Henry James, Iris Murdoch, than from some tactless older person's rebuke, whose intrusion and ill-temper we resent. The best fiction is a supplementary conscience, a further education, a sometimes disquieting emotional experience.

We can make some distinction, though one with blurred edges, many overlapping bits and many doubtful areas, between the greatest fiction, which gives an essentially true and illuminating picture of life, and the great mass of lesser fiction that belongs rather to the realm of organized, intelligent fantasy and is not much more than entertainment. When the good and brilliant Benjamin Jowett of Oxford wrote to a friend, 'There are few ways in which people can be better employed than in reading a good novel'[3] he was almost certainly thinking of the first category, something like *Adam Bede* or Tolstoy's *Resurrection*.

On the other hand, let us not be too priggish about those fictions that, nearer to mere fantasy, must be classed as 'escapist'. Pliny the Younger said that no book was so bad that some good could not be extracted from it. From light reading we may pick up a good many scraps of useful general knowledge and notions of lands, epochs, backgrounds and occupations different from our own; we may even find some sensible insights into character and motive and morality. In the detective tales of Arthur Conan Doyle, Dorothy Sayers, Agatha Christie, Ngaio Marsh, the police romances of John Creasey, even in the more callous thrillers of Ian Fleming, we may find nuggets of good sense, even of compassion, and reminders that our actions do affect other people. We are not mature readers until we can at least sense that George Eliot or Charles Dickens is much greater than Agatha Christie or Conan Doyle; and if we are serious students of literature we should be able to explain something of the distinction; but, other things being equal, the person whose reading never rises above the level of the better escapist fiction is likely to be better informed, better company, more tolerant and sympathetic and at least a little wiser than the person who never reads anything but a scrappy newspaper.

Moreover, need we totally scorn mere escapism? That person curled in an armchair with *The Clue of the Half-Baked Sausage Roll* may have been trying all day to teach negative or even aggressive pupils in an overcrowded school; made painfully uphill efforts as a probation officer to help the inadequate and the vicious; been doing the many unpleasant tasks a nurse has to do, among pain, fear and heavy responsibilities; or the trivial novel may be taking someone's mind off illness, injury, the loneliness of old age or the turmoil of adolescence. There are times when human beings need to put their feet up and relax.

A friend of mine, dying of cancer, had by his bed his Bible and the latest Agatha Christie. It was the Bible that really mattered to him; but if Agatha Christie can briefly distract someone in such a situation, she has not wasted her life. Mere entertainment does much to keep us sane, to provide a respite from reality that strengthens us to face it once more, and escapist literature at least does much to keep us out of mischief; the silliest, shallowest reader of something worthless is at least hurting nobody and giving no trouble. Yet great fiction, enlarging our awareness of human realities, can do much more for us than those lighter yarns we find easier to read but also easier to forget.

Should there be any censorship of literature? Totalitarian restriction of the exchange of ideas and information implies unreasoning tyranny and must be harmful to individual dignity and national civilization. But, just as some of our fantasies are downright beastly, some fiction may pander to our beastliest fantasies, and some people will supply anything for money.

It is odd that 'dirty books' mean books stimulating sexual desire, which may be linked with affection, kindness, gratitude; we are supposed to be scandalized more by pornography than by books instigating racial hatred, religious or political fanaticism, exaggerated nationalism, morbid fear, desolate cynicism, or contempt for human beings. Loathing hard-core pornography, I would still rather have *Fanny Hill* on my conscience than, say, *Mein Kampf* or a handbook on urban guerilla tactics. However, much pornography involves not friendly sex, but fantasies of hatred and degradation, and these might warp sexual feelings and make us less sensitive to the feelings of others. It is disquieting to know that when the totalitarian régime in Portugal fell in 1974 the police torturers were found to keep large stocks of pornographic magazines. It is also disquieting to ask ourselves who is wise and mature enough to be trusted with powers of censorship. I suspect that the best antidote to commercial pornography is the promotion of mental health and happy love, though that is more easily desired than achieved.

Can books put into people's heads ideas that are not at least almost there already? An insensitive oaf is not likely to read *Middlemarch*, let alone learn from it; a cool cerebral person may make little of D. H. Lawrence; I was not ripe to appreciate Henry James till I was over forty. The saddest thing about really evil books is that some people want them.

An account of lovely food may make me feel hungry. A fictional love scene may excite me; but most of us often feel hungry or sexy without the aid of books. No gloating over oysters would make me want one; no story about lesbians has ever stirred lesbian feeling in me. What a serious fictional treatment of lesbians can do for me is to show me how some women do love in this way, and can feel this as something complex, natural, partly unselfish, perhaps sacramental, as I feel heterosexual love. This is not depraving and corrupting me; it is enlightening and helping me; it is a moral gain to become kinder, more sympathetic and more informed about emotions we have not experienced. So serious literature should be allowed great freedom to treat all aspects of

8

experience and explore various interpretations of morality. A thoughtful study of even warped and repugnant emotions may give us insights into problems and force us to painful honesties of recognition, though insincere commercial pandering to them is vile.

We do not yet really know how far pornography may stimulate borderline cases to active wrongdoing and how far it may be a safety-valve. I object to it; but we must remember it is not the only unwholesome reading. Some types have been mentioned; but also the gentle, idealistic love romance that is misleadingly unreal about its happy ending may do harm by causing disastrously unreal expectations from marriage; religious books may arouse neurotic guilt instead of educating the conscience; much ordinary advertising appeals to ignoble feelings—with the greed, envy and competitiveness a good deal more harmful than the appeals to the sex interest.

Worthwhile fiction has at its best one great and splendid function: to strengthen our imaginative sympathies and insights and so make us wiser and better. It has, at many levels, the relatively trivial but genuinely useful function of providing comfort and amusement through fantasy; and these functions are seldom wholly separated. The chief form of printed fiction in Britain today is the novel.

The novel is the last major literary form to have developed. Literature of some sort was available in China as early as 1000 B.C.; the Sumerian *Epic of Gilgamesh* was composed about 1400 B.C.; Homer was writing his epics by the sixth century B.C.; but novels, as we understand the term, did not flourish in any quantity until the eighteenth century A.D.! There was plenty of fiction: epics, ballads, anecdotes, fables, folk-tales, myths, legends. There was some prose fiction: sagas in Iceland in the thirteenth century A.D.; in late Greek, *Daphnis and Chloe* by Longus (probably third century A.D.) and a few other short romances; in Latin, *The Golden Ass* of Apuleius (born *c.* A.D. 127); in Renaissance France, the stories of

Rabelais (? 1494–? 1553)—all still readable, but not novels as we should now define the term. English prose fictions, fore-runners of the novel rather than real novels, included the slow-moving *Euphues* (1578) by John Lyly; *Arcadia* (1590) by Sir Philip Sidney; *Rosalynde* (1590) by Thomas Lodge; later, in Aphra Behn's *Oroonoko* (1688) or William Congreve's *Incognita* (1692) there is some simple characterization. John Bunyan's wonderful *The Pilgrim's Progress* (1678) is of course allegorical, though with many touches of lifelike human observation. Some critics would class Daniel Defoe's *Robinson Crusoe* (1719) as the first real novel in English; others would specify Samuel Richardson's *Pamela* (1740).

No one can completely explain why the novel developed late and then flowed so copiously. Some of the causes may be: it is a form for solitary reading, so requires widespread literacy and leisure; it must have been helped by improved techniques of artificial lighting; it may have answered the new needs of a large middle class, of a society growing more specialized and complicated; it reflects an increasing conscious interest in psychology and sociology; the rise in the eighteenth century of commercial circulating libraries encouraged the professional novelist and today the public library system is still an important customer for new novels. There must be other factors.

What is a novel? There is no one clear definition accepted by all.

To Samuel Johnson, in his Dictionary of 1755, a novel was just 'A small tale, generally of love'. This will do for, say, *Rosalynde* or *Incognita*, but not for *Robinson Crusoe* (no love), or *Pamela* (not small) or *Joseph Andrews, Tom Jones, Peregrine Pickle*. Gradually the novel came to be taken more seriously, and is usually thought of as reaching the height of its dignity in the reign of Queen Victoria (1837–1901). The *Shorter Oxford English Dictionary* now defines it as 'A fictitious prose narrative of considerable length, in which characters and actions representative of real life are portrayed in a plot of more or less complexity.' *Webster's New Collegiate Dictionary* takes a similar view: 'An invented prose narrative that is usually long and complex and deals with human experience through a connected sequence of events.' So does *Cassell's English Dictionary*: 'A fictitious narrative in prose, usually of sufficient length to fill a volume, portraying characters and situations from real life.' The importance of character and relationship are stressed a little more in *Chambers Twentieth Century Dictionary*: 'A fictitious prose narrative or tale presenting a picture of real life, especially of the emotional crises in the life-history of the men and women portrayed'; and in *Collins's Dictionary*: 'A fictitious prose tale dealing with the adventures or feelings of imaginary persons so as to portray, by the description of action and thought, the varieties of human life and character.'

Now, these definitions, even the last, will include not only *Clarissa Harlowe, Tom Jones, Moll Flanders, Pride and Prejudice, Villette, Wuthering Heights, Vanity Fair, Daniel Deronda, Doctor Thorne, Tess of the D'Urbervilles, Ann Veronica, The Old Wives' Tale, The Wings of a Dove, Free Fall, The Masters* or *Lucky Jim*, but also *Ivanhoe, Frankenstein, The Woman in White, Westward Ho!, Lorna Doone, Treasure Island, The Hound of the Baskervilles, The Invisible Man, Kim, King Solomon's Mines* and perhaps even *The Nine Tailors* or *Goldfinger*; but many modern critics would put the first list in the class of novels and exclude the second.

The man in the street (or armchair) probably thinks of a novel as any long prose story. Public libraries often have one section for 'Fiction'—mostly somewhat serious novels—and separate sections for 'Mysteries', 'Westerns', and 'Science Fiction', three categories favoured by seekers of mere diversion, though a good novel is sometimes written in one of these genres.

However, as early as 1765 the *Complete Dictionary of Arts*

and Sciences (known as Croker's Dictionary) was making this distinction: 'NOVEL, in matters of literature, a fictitious history of a series of surprising and entertaining events in common life, wherein the rules of probability are or ought to be strictly preserved; in which it differs from a romance, where the hero and heroine is some prince or princess and the events which lead to the catastrophe in general highly absurd and unnatural.' Wyld's *Universal Dictionary of the English Language* (1936) defines the novel as 'A fictitious narrative (usually in prose) of some considerable length, representing human beings and their actions, adventures and passions, and displaying varieties of human character in relation to life; distinguished in the last feature from the older Romance.' Most critics today would probably insist that a true *novel* dealt above all with questions of *character, characters in relationship* and *cause and effect in relation to character.* A story of adventure with little interest in motives is a romance rather than a novel. Walter Allen in *The English Novel* (1954) sees the novel as 'a working model of life' as the novelist sees it.

Recently some critics have tried to narrow the definition still further; for example, to include in the true novel an element of 'education'; a character develops through learning more about life, such as Gwendolen in *Daniel Deronda*, Pip in *Great Expectations*, Elizabeth in *Pride and Prejudice*, Isabel in *Portrait of a Lady*, Sarah in Winifred Holtby's *South Riding* or Vic in Stan Barstow's *A Kind of Loving*. But do we count a novel in which the principal character has learned something, but not how to live more wisely, such as Henchard in *The Mayor of Casterbridge* or Paul in *Sons and Lovers*? And the good tale of detection includes a good deal of examination and reappraisal of characters and motives.

Northrop Frye[4] believes that 'novel' and 'romance' are always somewhat intermingled, and distinguishes four main types of fiction: *novel, confession, anatomy,* and *romance,* all of which may be found in one book. Perhaps we may say that the mainstream novel is a realistic fiction, enlarging our experience of life, rather than a fantasy transporting us to a more colourful world; but there can be no clear-cut distinction, and what one reader finds vividly realistic may seem to another too improbable to be real. It may muddle us more when we find that, whereas many critics exclude, say, *The Hound of the Baskervilles*, which *is* a tale about differentiated characters engaged in recognizable human activities in normal sequences of cause and effect, and relegate it to the category of romance, they will include in the History of the Novel such books as *Tristram Shandy*, *The Waves*, *At Swim-Two-Birds*, *Finnegans Wake* and *The Soft Machine*, which do *not* tell of characters interacting in normal sequences of cause and effect. Probably this is because such experimental works are recognized as having serious literary purpose, whereas a thriller, however craftsmanlike and consistent, is not meant to be taken seriously.

The purpose of this book is to help students of literature to read novels more analytically, both for enjoyment and for examinations; and for this purpose I shall take the *Shorter Oxford Dictionary* definition as sufficient. Now, this chapter has considered the meaning of *fiction*; we know *prose* is the opposite of *verse*; we will presently consider the *representation of real life*, of *character* and of cause and effect as *narrative*; but we are left with the *considerable length*.

How long is a novel? Longer than a short story. How long is a piece of string? We generally accept that a novel fills a volume, but 'How big is a book?' is not much more useful. There must be room for some complexity of plot and elaboration of character. E. M. Forster bravely ventured to suggest a minimum length of 50,000 words. (This book contains about 60,000.) There is no defined upper limit: there are novels of over a million words, such as *Clarissa Harlowe*; the longest novels are many-volume series, of which the longest is said to be Jules Romains's *Les Hommes de bonne volonté* in twenty-seven volumes; even among escapist romances we find Sergeanne Golon's *Angélique* in ten volumes. To give some idea of the size of a serious mainstream novel (as I shall call the kind of novel defined above): *The Heart of the Matter* contains about 59,000 words; *Jane Eyre*, about 107,000; *The Antiquary*, about 113,000; *Nostromo*, about 142,000; and *Middlemarch*, about 283,000.

Besides mentioning many novels, the following chapters will repeatedly refer to five particular novels; the reader may like to examine one of them more closely along the lines suggested:

Charles Dickens: *Hard Times* (1854)
George Eliot: *Silas Marner* (1861)
Henry James: *The Europeans* (1878)
Arnold Bennett: *Anna of the Five Towns* (1901)
Joseph Conrad: *The Secret Agent* (1907)

They all seem to me to be great novels; they are very different from one another; they are fairly short and simple; and all are easy to find.

2

VERISIMILITUDE

Pooh-Bah: Merely corroborative detail, intended to give artistic verisimilitude to an otherwise bald and unconvincing narrative.

W. S. Gilbert: *The Mikado*

Since the serious novel in some sense portrays real life, great effort goes into giving it verisimilitude, likeness to truth. We know the things did not happen, but must be made to feel that they could have happened. Since real life experience is not the same for us all, some people will find one novelist more convincingly true to life, others, another; and at any time anyone may have a new experience that will confirm or modify his opinion. I can see that the narrator in Soseki Natsume's *I am a Cat* is a very convincing cat, but cannot possibly judge the truthfulness of his portrayal of Japanese society.[1]

However, we can feel in general that the good mainstream novelist is intending to give some kind of true picture of life. He is something like a historian. A historian has to try to make a coherent, meaningful narrative of what, when people lived in it, seemed—and was—an enormous, ever-moving, endlessly interlinked, much misreported, bewildering flow of world events, charged with many contradictory emotions, muddled, illogical, never seen by anyone as a whole. Similarly, a novelist uses selection and pattern to try to make sense of the muddled turbulence or dreary chuggings of human life, and to give them a clear causal sequence. Most of us have small-scale experience of this: if I apply for a job with a *curriculum vitae*, this autobiography is truthful, but it comically simplifies my real, confused, overlapping, interlinking experience of life, and distorts the relative importance to me of my activities.

News reports are seldom trustworthy throughout; good reference books contain a few mistakes; we misremember our own past; present knowledge may be discredited by future discoveries; in one sense, all attempts to present 'truth' fail; but the novelist, like the conscientious historian, psychologist, sociologist or even scientist, tries to present at least some fragments of truth by applying imagination, insight and organization to observation.

Though we differentiate between the serious novel of character and motive, which keeps close to credible reality, and the romance with its less stern standards, we should remember that almost any fiction contains more reality than unreality, and we should remain fairly humble in our judgments on probability.

The most fantastic escapist stories depend on a certain ground of truth; in the wildest fantasy, our wonder depends on fact, for non-existent laws cannot be broken. H. G. Wells's *The Invisible Man* would make no sense if people could become invisible at will; Isaac Asimov's tales of humanoid robots depend for their impact on our knowledge of human motives and moral concepts. In the most far-fetched thriller, a man still falls down, bleeds blood, stops breathing when he dies.

We all need to remember almost continuously, not only in appraising novels, but in our whole approach to life and its problems, the extreme narrowness of our own experience. Modern communications and personal liberty have widened our first-hand experience as compared with that of a mediaeval peasant, but we still have very little. There is much truth in Rider Haggard's saying 'The story, on reflection, seemed to me utterly incredible, for I was not then old enough to be aware how many things happen in this world that the common sense of the average man would set down as so improbable as to be absolutely impossible.'[2]—or in Conan Doyle's 'My dear fellow, life is infinitely stranger than anything which the mind of man could invent. We would not dare to conceive the things which are really mere commonplaces of existence. If we could fly out of this window hand in hand, hover over this great city, gently remove the roofs, and peep in at the queer things which are going on, the strange coincidences, the plannings, the cross-purposes, the wonderful chains of events, working through generations, and leading to the most *outré* results, it would make all fiction with its conventionalities and foreseen conclusions most stale and unprofitable'[3]—although the first leads up to a story almost certainly impossible, and the second to one that is improbable, though possible. Life, as well as fiction, contains coincidences, grave results from trifling accidents, mistakes of identity, prodigious villainies and heroic loyalties, physical and mental endurances, injustices arising from misleading appearances or elaborate deceits, obsessive and disproportionate passions, crippling remorses, incongruous mixtures of good and evil in one person, enormous absurdities, accumulations of disaster or good luck, strange secrets and astounding revelations. Any number of the *News of the World* contains, even allowing for some mistakes in reporting, material a skilled novelist could work up into excellent sensational stories, or even into great novels.

When at eighteen I heard some woman object to a novel she was reading on the grounds that its heroine, in middle life and a responsible post, could not 'have time' for falling in love, I was ignorant enough to believe her, though sadly. Now life has shown me that she was just dogmatizing on narrow experience. We may often find too improbable something in a novel, when another person can parallel it with an incident from real life.

What real life lacks are not the oddities, incongruities,

sensational elements and strange motives often found in novels, but the pattern, coherence and sense of perspective imposed by the novelist's selection and explanation.

Some readers criticize *Jane Eyre* for its improbabilities, and despise it as the mere wishful fantasy of a lonely woman. There is one inartistically crude improbability: when Jane collapses exhausted on a doorstep and that very house contains three unknown cousins. But when we are told that Mr Rochester is an inexperienced girl's picture of a dominant male—true enough—and that he is modelled on Lord Byron, we do need also to remember that Lord Byron was a real live person, in many ways a more 'improbable' person leading a more 'improbable' life than the imagined Edward Rochester. In *The Antiquary*, Lord Glenallan ruined his health by remorse for a sin he was tricked into thinking he had committed, and by severe penances: the history of religion records many such obsessions of expiation in real life. Charles Reade amassed documentary sources for most of the sensational scenes in his novels. The sufferings depicted in B. Traven's *The Death Ship* and *The Rebellion of the Hanged*, or by Harriet Beecher Stowe in *Uncle Tom's Cabin*, were described in order to expose real abuses.

In *Vanity Fair* the devotion of Captain Dobbin to the sweet ninny Amelia may seem overdone, until we see some example of such patient loyalty to a rather inadequate object in real life. By the age of forty most of us have probably met at least one person who is slogging out a life half spoilt in generous affection for some weaker person. Can any fictional wickedness seem implausible when we know there have recently been conferences of professional torturers, and Northern Ireland, Vietnam, Bangladesh and Cyprus are only a few examples of what human beings will do to one another?

Sometimes what looks implausible seems so to us because of social changes, as when in the Conan Doyle story quoted above the brilliant Holmes says, 'I believe a single lady can

get on very nicely upon an income of about sixty pounds'
(i.e. for a year!). But this was in about 1861. There must be
hundreds of novels in which the plot depends on a valuation
of chastity which even a practising Christian would nowadays
think exaggerated. Maggie in *The Mill on the Floss* is utterly
disgraced for an indiscretion hardly anyone would think of
as in the least wrong today; most of us want to kick her
brother Tom for turning her out; but, while we are meant to
sympathize more with Maggie, in her day Tom too had a
case of some sort. A home like that in Samuel Butler's *The
Way of All Flesh* would today be seen as a horrible freak, not
as a fairly ordinary state of affairs.

Class distinctions have long been disappearing, blurring or
shifting. We may still over-value money, perhaps over-value
youth, but few now over-value pedigree. Jane Austen was
notably sensible and shrewd, but today we have to do some
sympathetic time-travelling to understand her preoccupations
with contrasts of good breeding and vulgarity, whereas her
more important contrasts of kindness and callousness,
integrity and hypocrisy, considerateness with selfishness, ring
true at once.

In her *Mansfield Park*, a private production of *Lovers' Vows*[4]
is a touchstone: the wise and well behaved characters deplore
the choice of play and the head of the house is much dis-
pleased when he hears of it. This sounds as if *Lovers' Vows*
were coarse or immoral; but it is a rhetorical, sentimental
drama in which an illegitimate son meets his father and
wrongs are righted; it stresses responsibility and family
affection; the difficulty today would be that it is so solemnly
moral that the audience might snigger in the wrong place.
Yet there is no doubt that the sensible, balanced Jane Austen
assumes we shall be on the side of those who disapprove.
Again, in Trollope's *Doctor Thorne* Frank Gresham soundly
horsewhips a mercenary cad who has jilted Frank's sister;
though the thrashing is in some sense earned, we have to

make some effort of imagination to accept that Frank's father was 'well pleased' and that Frank went unpunished except for a short period of police surveillance.

Even in reading a contemporary novel, we may have to enter imaginatively into styles of life well outside what we ourselves take for granted. However, a novel cannot enlarge our sympathies unless the novelist does in most respects achieve verisimilitude. How is this done?

Some novelists have given great attention to how the story came to be told. Richardson's *Pamela* is told in a series of letters, mostly from the heroine. He incorporates the letter-writing into the plot with care, treating of such problems as paper supplies, delivery and delays; but the device of telling the tale in letters has a negative as well as a positive effect: how did a young woman, first a hard-working servant, then in captivity, then a busy wife, ever write all those letters—and with a quill pen at that? *Clarissa* and Fanny Burney's *Evelina* are also told in letters. Nathaniel Hawthorne introduced his stark, concentrated *The Scarlet Letter* with a rather tedious forty-page prelude explaining how the story reached him. *The Pickwick Papers* starts as the record of a social club, though this device is soon forgotten. In Henry Treece's *Electra* the dying heroine talks to the doctor attending her. Yet the question of where the story comes from has probably worried the novelist more than the reader, who seems quite happy just to accept it as a literary convention; most novels do in fact step directly into narrative without much machinery.

What is important in all mainstream novels is not special contrivances for pretending the novel is fact, but verisimilitude in the story itself: not evidence that the events did happen, when we know they did not, but the portrayal of events we feel could happen.

On the lower levels the novelist achieves this chiefly by close observation and by collecting information: here memory is important. Some novelists keep notebooks to help their memories. Details of the external world will be made as accurate as possible. There is the world of nature: seasons, climates, flora, fauna, sickness and health, seas, skies, woods, hills, gardens; the world of man-made objects: costume, food, houses, furniture, equipment, transport, weapons, apparatus, shops and their contents; the world of society: social dependencies and activities, manners and customs, organizations, politics, law, committees, religious institutions, education, class relationships. Many minor novelists have shown a respectable talent for choosing and presenting convincing details. Angela Thirkell commands some happy phrasing for the small crises of domestic life and minor problems of social occasions; Ian Fleming at his best gives sharp pictures of places, meals and exotic oddities. The police yarns of John Creasey or suspense stories of Arthur Hailey sustain their illusion mostly by accumulations of authentic technical detail. On a higher level, C. P. Snow gains much of his credibility from the details of worlds he knows from inside: institutions and committee-work. Ernest Hemingway and Kingsley Amis, in their very different ways, gain many of their most memorable effects from the concise convincingness of details we can visualize—whether the routines of a hunter or soldier, or the concealment of a burned bed-sheet. D. H. Lawrence supports his primary concern with emotions and relationships by vivid details of nature and atmosphere.

Dickens has a genius for the telling detail; the reader may think of Mrs Sparsit's 'gritty mittens' and examine his details of Coketown or the countryside, or just some brilliant touch like these lines on Mrs Sparsit, spying on Louisa in a wood:

> Mrs Sparsit's white stockings were of many colours, green predominating; prickly things were in her shoes; caterpillars slung themselves, in hammocks of their own making, from various parts of her dress; rills ran from her bonnet, and her Roman nose.

Verisimilitude

George Eliot does not have quite Dickens's relish for concrete details, but when she needs them she uses them very cleverly, as when Silas finds Eppie

> discoursing cheerfully to her own small boot, which she was using as a bucket to convey the water into a deep hoof-mark while her little naked foot was planted comfortably on a cushion of olive-green mud. A red-headed calf was observing her with alarmed doubt through the opposite hedge.

Henry James makes comparatively little use of concrete details and practical activities; he is a specialist in shades of feeling and motive; but he can set a scene, and with great economy, when he wishes:

> She passed slowly downstairs, still looking about. The broad staircase made a great bend, and in the angle was a high window, looking westward, with a deep bench, covered with a row of flowering plants in curious old pots of blue China-ware. The yellow afternoon light came in through the flowers and flickered a little on the white wainscots. Eugenia paused a moment; the house was perfectly still, save for the ticking, somewhere, of a great clock. The lower hall stretched away at the foot of the stairs, half covered over with a large Oriental rug.

Arnold Bennett treats concrete detail rather more as Dickens does. When we see the Tellwright family at breakfast on Anna's birthday, we see details that vividly convey the joyless, loveless monotony and ugliness of life in that home. The six pieces of bacon, of which Mr Tellwright eats three, are only one example. In even fewer words, Conrad on his first page gives us the feel of Verloc's nasty little shop, a mere cover for his real, secret activities.

Brilliant though such detail can be, it remains on the lower levels of verisimilitude. The credibility, though not the subtlety, is often found in stories of little literary merit; indeed, commercial storytellers often do a good deal of genuine research and observation. One of the main differences between light reading and great literature is that in the latter another level of truth to life is reached, beyond the concrete and practical. There is a quest for truth in the realms of psychology and morality; motives, emotional complexities, moral development, interplay of character and emotion; our self-deceptions and our slow evolutions towards an awareness of self and others; questions of purpose, of principle, of the deeper reaches of the conflict of good and evil; truth in portraying something of the tangled, inexhaustible complexity of our emotional, moral, social and spiritual being and its relationship with others.

Great literature is not only harder to write, but harder to read. The hero of an adventure story is usually up against either a well defined villain whom it is plainly meritorious to thwart, or some task or hazard. Very different demands are made on Dorothea Casaubon in *Middlemarch* or Maggie Ververs in *The Golden Bowl*. The literature that forces us to look into ourselves is harder to read than the stories that take us out of ourselves; but in the long run it gives greater rewards.

Concrete detail itself may often have some moral or symbolic significance in addition to its obvious practical interest. When Stephen Blackpool left Mr Bounderby's house, after hearing his marital tragedy dismissed with sickening insensitivity, he

> descended the two white steps, shutting the black door with the brazen door-plate, by the aid of the brazen full stop, to which he gave a parting polish with the sleeve of his coat, observing that his hot hand clouded it.

Here is a hint of Stephen's sensitive consideration for others, but also a poetic aptness: the black and brazen door suggests

Bounderby's black and brazen soul and perhaps its being closed to any awareness of others with compassion or even tolerance.

In Oliver Schreiner's *The Story of an African Farm*, the children, Lyndall, of enquiring mind, and Em, of quieter temperament, are locked in their bedroom after an altercation over the treatment of an old shepherd. Lyndall makes resourceful attempts to break the window and shutters, or burn her way out; Em watches and weeps. The concrete details are vivid, but the episode also foreshadows Lyndall's brave, tragic adult life; she tries to break out of her ignorant, stifling background, shows courage and resource, but is defeated and broken. Em too shows character, but in a much quieter way. In John Wain's *A Winter in the Hills* the hero, driven from his lodgings, camps for a time in a disused chapel. A lot of detail about the business of lighting the stove and looking after it gives authenticity—a practical problem has to be solved—but the stove also suggests the family hearth and warmth of heart, and the novel tells how Roger Furnivall develops in responsibility and generous affection until he is even prepared to take on two stepchildren with the woman he loves. In Iris Murdoch's *A Fairly Honourable Defeat*, Hilda, third victim of a cruel trick that has led her husband and her friend into a destructive love-situation, learns the truth and at once tries to telephone her husband. Vivid details of how she breaks the telephone and it disintegrates are frighteningly real; but, again, the mishap is a kind of metaphor for what has happened: a useful instrument of communication (letters) betrays the user and so becomes negative, grotesque, terrifying.

Yet the greatest verisimilitudes of the greatest novels are their insights into the human heart: society and its demands; human beings in relation to family, friends and others; human beings in the ultimate loneliness of individuality. There is moral truth, in the sense that laws and principles apply in our lives, even though we are not all agreed about all questions of morality, especially in specific situations; if we always knew what was right, there would be no dilemmas, only efforts; in great literature we do often recognize, not so much fundamental truths, perhaps, as certain fundamental moral probabilities: for instance, that much of a worthwhile life is our learning to shoulder the right responsibilities, sometimes while repudiating the wrong ones; or that respect for the other personality is an essential part of any good relationship; or that we need to keep a careful watch on our own capacity for justifying whatever suits us best; or deeper and stranger mysteries of self-discovery, reconciliation or redemption; the nature of freedom, the learning of humility and compassion, the unlearning of self-hatred, the finding of purposes, the generosities and healing sacraments of love, the recognition of our real aloneness. We need be committed to no church to find some ring of reality in Mrs Winthrop's provisional and homely answer to Silas Marner:

> And all as we've got to do is to trusten, Master Marner—
> to do the right things as fur as we know, and to trusten.
> For if us as knows so little can see a bit o' good and rights,
> we may be sure as there's a good and rights bigger nor
> what we can know—I feel it in my own inside as it must
> be so.

Or, though there could scarcely be a novelist of standing who was much further in tone and temper from George Eliot than is Kingsley Amis, there are the lovers in *I Want It Now*, two people appallingly selfish, ruthless and dishonest, who work their way through some glimmers of sincerity and rudiments of love to a policy of helping each other to be a little less bad than either is alone.

For this kind of moral truth the reader may look again at poor, silly, fussy, boring Mrs Gradgrind on her deathbed, fumbling after the imagination and affection that her husband had, in his very irrational kind of rationalism, denied; or look again at the crucial interview in *Silas Marner*, in which Godfrey confesses to his wife Nancy that Eppie is his child, and the wife's reaction is more generous than he expected, yet quietly firm: 'I wasn't worth doing wrong for—nothing is in this world.'

In *The Europeans*, in which the contrast between calculating worldly policy about marriage and the growth of spontaneous affection is an important theme, there is a bright moment when Mr Brand, who has long paid court to Gertrude, intervenes to ask the father to consent to her marrying Felix, then expresses his wish to conduct that ceremony. This gesture brings in a higher level of motive, and its romantic or dramatic element contrasts with Mr Wentworth's slow, pompous insensitivity. Henry James lived too late and knew too much to keep this as just a noble gesture, as it could have been for Walter Scott or Charlotte Brontë; even the young couple perceive some ambiguity:

'That was a fine stroke,' said Felix. 'It was really heroic.'

Gertrude sat musing, with her eyes upon the ripples. 'That was what he wanted to be; he wanted to do something fine.'

'He won't be comfortable till he has married us', said Felix. 'So much the better.'

'He wanted to be magnanimous; he wanted to have a fine moral pleasure. I know him so well', Gertrude went on. Felix looked at her; she spoke slowly, gazing at the clear water. 'He thought of it a great deal, night and day. He thought it would be beautiful. At last he made up his mind that it was his duty, his duty to do just that—nothing less than that. He felt exalted; he felt sublime. That's how he likes to feel. It is better for him than if I had listened to him.'

That Mr Brand is of a temperament that finds much satisfaction in behaving handsomely does not alter the fact that he has behaved handsomely; after all, there are many worse temperaments; but it may perhaps be said that a large part of the moral truth of many twentieth-century novels is the increasing awareness of such moral ambiguities, subtler than the self-deceptions so brilliantly demonstrated by George Eliot, or the inner conflicts of passion or pride with virtue that are so vivid and vehement in Charlotte Brontë's heroines. But, with all the ambiguities of Henry James or Herman Melville, Saul Bellow or Virginia Woolf, the excitement of moral and psychological insights is still there in a modified form.

One of many masterstrokes in *Anna of the Five Towns* comes when Anna has just accepted Mynors's offer of marriage: 'She saw pictures of her career as his wife, and resolved that one of the first acts of her freedom should be to release Agnes from the more ignominious of her father's tyrannies.' Bennett adds no comment; but this shows that Anna's docility in her hard life is resigned, not blind; she lives mostly in a spirit of unselfish love; and through this delight in the hope of helping her sister we are also shown that, though compared with Anna's father Mynors is an angel of release, Anna has no real love–joy in him; even her marriage must be part of her effort to do the best she can, not an eager doing of what she most wants. She has been nurtured with such stifling callousness that she can hardly even desire any real personal fulfilment.

Repeatedly in *The Secret Agent*, a story of heroic sacrifices made vain by human folly and evil, Conrad shows us the pathos of ineffective goodness in the mentally defective Stevie, who cannot bear the sufferings of others, but cannot even articulate his protests. In the episode of the cab journey we are shown, through the eyes of a youth of low intelligence, a problem that puzzles the greatest minds: the way in which suffering, and causing to suffer, seem woven into the very fabric of life, even without anyone's conscious malice. All

Stevie can say is 'Bad! Bad!' and feel a dim longing to comfort the horse and the cabman like children in his bed.

No novel can give any 'total truth', any more than any man-devised religion, philosophy or political theory can do so; but a good novel leaves us with some sense of fragmentary truthfulness; and a great novel gives us a very complex, very multiple impression of a portion of life and its problems, communicating many diverse insights, some explicitly, some by implication. The great novelist has both to be sincere—to be genuinely wanting to tell the truth—and to achieve verisimilitude—to enable the reader to believe in his truthfulness. We know from common experience that these are not the same: most of us have met plausible liars and have also been suspected of lying when we were telling the truth. Technical skill may not make us sincere, but it is needed to communicate; and the remainder of this book will mostly be dealing with the necessary techniques, with special reference to plot, characters, conversation and background. One matter, however, needs attention first; the question of who is telling the tale, and the relation of this to truth and verisimilitude. For some measure of credibility in this very existence of the story is obviously important.

3

THE POINT OF VIEW

All bodies are confined within some place,
But she all place within herself confines;
All bodies have their measure and their space,
But who can draw the Soul's dimensive lines?

No *body* can at once two forms admit,
Except the one the other do deface;
But in the Soul ten thousand forms do sit,
And none intrudes into her neighbour's place.

Sir John Davies (1569–1629): *Nosce Teipsum*

Stories do not tell themselves; whoever is telling a story has to be somewhere in relation to the story, in order to tell it. Once we have got beyond the distinction, learned in childhood, between a true story, an imagined story, and a lie, we seem to accept the convention of fiction without fuss. The answer to the question, 'Have you heard the one about the giraffe that found a pair of tights?' may be, 'No, do tell it', or 'Yes, I heard it from Sid', or even 'I don't care for that sort of story!'—but it is never, 'How do you come to be telling it?' We do not mind where the novelist stands, but he has to stand somewhere, either in the scene or outside it. He may also change his point of view; but at any particular moment he must have one.

Any point of view is to some extent exclusive. However much you can see from your front bedroom window, you cannot see what is behind the house. Even when you see whole counties at once from an aeroplane, you do not then

29

see the delphiniums in a front garden. The novelist may choose to examine a small portion of experience closely, like Jane Austen, Virginia Woolf or James Joyce, or a larger field with less minute detail, like Dickens or Tolstoy or Pasternak. One novelist may of course write several novels with different perspectives: for instance, Arnold Bennett's *Riceyman Steps* has four important characters and a simple plot, its merits being those of concentration and intensity; his *The Old Wives' Tale* has a large cast, varied scenes, much more placing of the story in a framework of history and politics, a longer time-scale and a more complex plot, so that its merits arise from larger scope and the placing of vividly portrayed individuals in a huge panorama of the passing years. The burning-glass concentration of Alexander Solzhenitsyn's *One Day in the Life of Ivan Denisovich* involves a technique very different from the complexity and multiplicity of his *The First Circle*.

There are as many points of view as there are novels, but the novelist has three basic methods for taking up a position, together with a rare fourth method, if for the present we leave out some of the more extreme experimental techniques. He can tell the story essentially from the point of view of one person, either by impersonating that person and writing as 'I' or by following the person through his adventures and writing of 'He'. He can tell the story as an omniscient narrator, choosing to recount what he thinks of interest, but implying that he knows a great deal more about all the characters and incidents, more than anyone could know in real life, for he knows the motives of any number of characters, and in real life we have a rather poor grasp of even our own! He can tell the story from several points of view, either by impersonating a number of people in succession, or by following several of them in succession. Rarely, he may pretend not to be there at all, presenting the reader with what purports to be objective evidence, such as a file of documents, without comment.

The point of view

All methods may be combined in one novel; indeed, some variation of viewpoint is not only usual, but, in a mainstream novel, almost inevitable, in that someone is at some time going to put his own side of a case or relate some experience as he experienced it.

When an observer takes up his position on a hill to watch a scene and report, he may not always keep his eyes front, stare at the scene and keep his commentary in the same style throughout. He may pick up binoculars and focus them on something for a while, then put them down; he may turn to us, prod someone in the chest and make a comment— Fielding, Charlotte Brontë or Thackeray, for instance, may address the 'Reader' now and then; he may withdraw his gaze from the broad scene to examine a flower or beetle; sing a song; interrupt his examination of the scene to make a weather forecast; signal to some friend stationed at another observation post;[1] meditate or daydream; he may even suddenly stand on his head, turn a somersault, or fire a rocket from which twenty little frogs with pink spots presently float down under bright yellow nylon parachutes. The language of his reports, too, may range from the easiest plain language to the most personal idiom or even to difficult codes.

Most mainstream novels are written from the point of view of an omniscient, or at least very well informed, narrator, who follows either one character, or several. Readers do not mind this; in fact most of us find it the easiest kind of novel to follow; but novelists have often been uneasy about the convention. Henry James was uncomfortable about what he called 'the mere muffled majesty of irresponsible author-ship' and preferred the point of view of 'some more or less detached, some not strictly involved, though thoroughly interested and intelligent witness or reporter, some person who contributes to the case mainly a certain amount of criticism and interpretation of it'.[2] Experiments in approach have continued ever since the beginnings of the English novel, although in the twentieth century more drastic innovations have been tried.

What may be reckoned the first major English novels were told from one point of view, or at least from one for most of the time: Defoe's *Robinson Crusoe* (1719), *Moll Flanders* (1722), *Colonel Jack* (1722), and Richardson's *Pamela* (1740) have each a single point of view involving impersonation. Robinson Crusoe tells his own story and Colonel Jack his, in simple, straightforward language which can be felt as suitable to men of intelligence but little education. Of course such men would not really have had the verbal mastery to write such lucid, economical stories: when we remember what an effort it is for most people to write even short letters, we see that any such impersonation is very much a literary convention. In *Moll Flanders* Defoe tries the harder task of impersonating a woman, and does adopt a rather feminine tone and different style. Richardson's *Pamela* has already been mentioned; Pamela tells her own story in letters, though a few other people contribute isolated extra letters.

Fielding in *Joseph Andrews* (1742) does not impersonate, but as an omniscient narrator tells the story of Joseph; he follows the fortunes of Joseph and Parson Adams, with some pauses to follow Fanny and others, and the tale of Leonora, which almost stands by itself, as a variant. He adopts much the same method in *Tom Jones* (1749), following Tom, Sophia and sometimes other persons. These novels do not have a single point of view, but in both the greater part of the attention is given to the hero. Fielding has a good many self-conscious digressions about literary and other problems, interesting as critical comment but slowing the story; and in both his best known novels there are elements of parody: of *Pamela* in *Joseph Andrews*; of the epic tradition in *Tom Jones*. Apart from this, Fielding sets a general pattern for the most usual type of English mainstream novel: the narrator follows

one or more of his characters through the plot, with any
explanations he thinks necessary.

In *Amelia* (1751) Fielding uses multiple points of view: the
story is begun by an unidentified narrator, who brings
together, in prison, Miss Matthews and Mr Booth; Miss
Matthews tells her story and then Mr Booth his; some
straight narrative follows, until Mrs Bennet tells her sad story
to Amelia; then Fielding resumes his straight narrative.

An early example of pretended objectivity is Smollet's *The
Expedition of Humphry Clinker*, which purports to be a
collection of letters from various persons, collected by the
Reverend Jonathan Dustwich and relating to a journey to
Scotland. The letters need no further narrative or commentary: characters reveal themselves through the content and
style, even the spelling; though to some extent Mr Melford,
a moderate, sensible man, acts as a narrator. The story is thin;
the charm of the book is in comic incidents and contrasts of
character.

Experiment going beyond these fairly obvious conventions
also began in the early days of the English novel with Sterne's
Tristram Shandy (published in successive volumes, 1760–7),
which is not a narrative at all as we ordinarily understand the
term.

Impersonating one character, narrating as 'I', can give great
vitality and conviction; the difficulty is that the restriction to
one point of view very much limits the field that can be
observed. However, this, besides increasing intensity, may
well heighten the sense of reality, in that we all experience life
through one pair of eyes only. Anyone who has made any effort
towards true love, true friendship or even good professional
relationships knows how hard it is to come anywhere near
putting ourselves imaginatively in the other person's place.

An impersonation may be sympathetic, or ironical, or a
mixture of both. Jane Eyre, and Lucy Snowe in *Villette*, tell
their stories as women of character, sensitive, observant,

sensible and good; this is partly because their stories represent some of Charlotte Brontë's own experiences and longings, so that she may to some extent have identified herself with them. Certainly she invites the reader to do so. David Copperfield tells his own story with a similar effect, for similar reasons. Herman Melville's *Moby Dick* is related not by the 'hero', Captain Ahab, but by the one survivor of the *Pequod*, who begins, 'Call me Ishmael'. He is a straight character, telling the story as a sensible, sympathetic, awed but often ironical observer, though his amazing style cannot be taken as a realistic imitation of an uneducated sailor's diction. The American lieutenant who tells his story of love and war in Hemingway's *A Farewell to Arms* is given a diction more suitable to the impersonated character, a kind of stylized inarticulateness. In H. G. Wells's *Tono-Bungay* the hero, George Ponderevo, describes his own life; he begins by saying that he is not a novelist, but an engineer trying to tell a story. C. P. Snow tells several stories through a participant, Lewis Eliot.

One of the greatest of ironical impersonations is Mark Twain's *Huckleberry Finn*. This novel is a greater sequel to *Tom Sawyer*. Huck tells his own story, in his own unacademic language and with his own views on life. We are not expected to take him entirely seriously:

I've always reckoned that looking at the new moon over your left shoulder is one of the carelessest and foolishest things a body can do. Old Hank Bunken done it once, and bragged about it; and in less than two years he got drunk and fell off the shot-tower and spread himself out so that he was just a kind of layer, as you may say; and they slid him edgeways between two barn doors for a coffin, and buried him so, so they say, but I didn't see it. Pap told me. But anyway, it all comes of looking at the moon that way, like a fool.

Huck's notions of cosmogony are no more scientific than his theory of causality:

> We had the sky, up there, all speckled with stars, and we used to lay on our backs and look up at them, and discuss about whether they was made, or only just happened— Jim he allowed they was made, but I allowed they happened; I judged it would have took too long to *make* so many. Jim said the moon could a *laid* them; well, that looked kind of reasonable, so I didn't say nothing against it, because I've seen a frog lay most as many, so of course it could be done.

His ideas of civilization, morality and religion are deliciously muddled; but this does not just amuse us; it gives Mark Twain a device for the ironical consideration of slavery and some of the follies of 'wiser' people.

In *Wife to Mr Milton* Robert Graves makes Milton's uncongenial first wife, Mary Powell, put her own point of view. The impression is clever, plausible and sympathetic, but contains a tremendous irony: the bewildered woman, victim of Milton's rare kind of egoism, has no awareness that she is married to one of the greatest of all English poets. It is her own quite natural sense of herself as the centre of things that gives the book its ironical originality. In Daniel Keyes's *Flowers for Algernon*, a science-fiction novel of some depth, Charlie Gordon, a good-natured moron, becomes an experimental subject for a scientist who has a method for artificially increasing intelligence. Charlie is given intelligence far above average and then an excellent intensive education. As his intellect develops he also comes to understand emotional problems better; but the change does not last; his intelligence declines and at the end of the story he is again a humble, good-natured moron who dimly remembers that he was once a genius. The impersonation follows him in his first-person story from his first misspelt, muddled report through growing articulateness to sophisticated self-analysis and contributions to scientific thought, then back down the other side, the last lines being misspelt, muddled and full of dignified pathos.

When the author is following a main character and telling the story in the third person, there may be still a measure of actual impersonation. In Hemingway's *The Old Man and the Sea* or Henry Treece's *The Dream-Time*, a great simplicity of language suits the primitive characters; in contrast, Saul Bellow, following Asa Leventhal, who is a minor professional editor, through *Victim*, uses a more sophisticated style. But a third-person following of a character does not always include any imitation of the person's style of thinking: for instance, Joyce Cary, in *A Fearful Joy*, follows the valiant, ill-used Tabitha with great compassion but also a detachment that allows of rather clinical comments and good-natured ironies. Somerset Maugham in *Liza of Lambeth* follows Liza with a dry detachment; he hardly explains at all; he tells us what she does; and the cool observation in fact lets us see not only Liza's ignorance, vulgarity and folly, but her gleams of nobility: her gallant high spirits, her confused aspirations to decency and even dignity, her stoical goodness to her selfish, drunken mother. Sinclair Lewis does something similar, though with heavier, more obvious, ironies, in his *Babbitt*, in which life is seen through the experience of an American businessman, philistine, self-deluding, emotionally stunted. As in *Liza of Lambeth*, commentaries would weaken the sense of reality; but the clear ironies let Babbitt appear, by the end of the novel, as not only disgusting, but somewhat pathetic—somewhere in his shrunken, trashy, synthetic soul a few dim gropings after goodness still twitch. We are made to loathe him, but also to doubt if he can help being what he is. By keeping to Babbitt's own point of view in his endless self-deceptions, Lewis makes us see a little of ourselves in them. H. G. Wells, following Kipps or Mr Polly, lets us see what they saw, and combines a quasi-scientific detachment with warm sympathy, so that we feel the absurdity of the characters, yet like them and see that they not only could hardly help being so daft, but were indeed doing their brave bests in a world more viciously daft.

It is also possible for a novelist to follow one character for his point of view, without making us sympathize with that character. Kingsley Amis in *One Fat Englishman* makes us see through the eyes of Roger Micheldene, even feel some of his distresses; but shows Roger as immensely selfish, self-indulgent, impatient, and very intolerant of the frailties of everyone else, even of their mere differences of taste or personality from his own. William Golding, in *Pincher Martin*, follows, except in one last chapter, the point of view of the dying Christopher Hadley Martin, another nasty specimen.

A single fictitious point of view need not necessarily be human. In *Flush* Virginia Woolf tells the story of the Browning marriage from the point of view of Elizabeth's spaniel; in *White Fang* Jack London tells the story of a wolf-dog from its own point of view; Paul Gallico's *Jennie* follows a small boy who for most of the time is a cat. Science fiction attempts sometimes to tell stories from viewpoints other than human: A. E. Van Vogt's *Slan*, with its telepath hero and heroine, is a half-way example.

The omniscient narrator, who in a large majority of novels is the actual teller of the story, may follow any number of characters for short or long sections of the book, tell what he thinks is most interesting and comment if he wishes. He often gives a large share of the attention to one character, but sometimes turns aside to follow another. Graham Greene follows Scobie through most of *The Heart of the Matter*, but Scobie is not present throughout. Most of Vladimir Nabokov's *Pnin* is told from the point of view of Professor Pnin, a Russian refugee with a flair for wrong decisions; but a longish section follows his ex-wife's son, other points of view are taken briefly, and the last chapter is told as by another Russian.

Often the omniscient narrator is not following any one character, but, as it were, standing back from all the characters, observing and reporting. He usually shows more sympathy with some than with others, and makes some more important than others, but keeps a measure of detachment. Dickens, except in *David Copperfield*, usually adopts this method: for instance, in *Nicholas Nickleby* he has many scenes in which Nicholas plays no part and about which he cannot know. This also exemplifies an important advantage the omniscient narrator has: he can show us some plan, plot or problem and let us watch with excitement as the other characters move towards it. Again, we can enjoy the ridiculous rather more when we are not invited to identify too closely with one character: if Dickens followed Kate Nickleby as closely as Charlotte Brontë follows Caroline Helstone in parts of *Shirley*, we might feel Kate's humiliation and handicap by her mother's silly loquacity too much to relish the skill with which Mrs Nickleby's unreason, muddle and self-deluding self-importance are portrayed.

In *Heart of Midlothian* Scott's sympathy is clearly with Jeanie Deans, and for some pages at a time he does follow her closely, but he also portrays a wide variety of scenes and persons, with much commentary. His apparent objectivity does not chill the atmosphere: the trial, one of the finest things in the book, might be less credible if we saw it through Jeanie's or Effie's eyes. Scott, keeping at a distance, is able to show physical details of the scene, to contrast the cool rational manner of the lawyers and the judge with the intense emotions of the two girls and their father, and even to add a few comic touches. The use of the Books of Adjournal, repeating Effie's statements, paradoxically deepen the pathos; Effie's words are reported in the formal, prescribed manner for such documents, but the personality and anguish force their way through:

Interrogated, if it died a natural death after birth? Declares, not to her knowledge. Interrogated, where it now is? Declares, she would give her right hand to ken, but that she never hopes to see mair than the banes of it. And being interrogated, why she supposes it is now dead? the declarant wept bitterly, and made no answer.

In Stephen Crane's *The Red Badge of Courage* or Hemingway's *For Whom the Bell Tolls*, the writers remain close to their central characters, and we see war as terrible, but individual man as retaining some dignity and significance. In Joseph Heller's *Catch-22* one character, Yossarian, plays a greater part than the others, but, except for a few passages—notably a serious one near the end—he and all the characters are seen from a distance; we are jolted from one eccentric character, one incident of wild unreason, one crazy conversation, to another; the narrator just invites us to observe the whole panorama of waste, absurdity, callousness and fraud with scientific interest. The individuals are not given enough importance to make us care about their survival; it is the total mess that has vitality, like a heap of maggots under a lens.

This omniscient narrator can comment on anything he likes to comment on; he can analyse motives more objectively than a character can; he can describe things no other person could really see, such as a man's terrors in solitary confinement, or a dream; he can set persons in a historical or sociological perspective with a grasp of essentials impossible to a person living through the events; he can relate characters and events to things that have not yet happened; he can throw in any cultural allusions his readers are likely to enjoy, and even, as Dickens often does, have jokes with the reader at the expense of the characters. He can contribute his own moral values, explicitly or by implication. He has the greatest freedom; his is the viewpoint of a wide-angled lens. The single point of view has the intensity of a close-up lens, but its field must be restricted.

Telling a story from several points of view has obvious possibilities for representing characters in depth, or the ambiguities of life; it can thus add verisimilitude, contribute large-scale ironies, and perhaps give the relief of variety.

All dialogue involves tiny multiple impersonations; but multiple impersonations on a big scale are rarer: an example is John Wain's *Strike the Father Dead*, in which the story is taken up by three people in turn: Alfred, the father, a narrow-minded professor of classics whose mind has hardened into crippling dogmatism, but who was once himself in revolt against a dogmatic father and in need of understanding; Eleanor, his sister, a loving, unselfish woman, a peacemaker and a woman of common sense; Jeremy, the rebellious son, with an artist's attitude to his jazz, a streak of critical cynicism, no appreciation of his father's values, and a good heart. One of the merits of this novel is that all are shown as having some merit in their values; the pathos arises because they are all aiming at the good, in their different ways, but cannot communicate. Each character is given a prose style suited to age, mode of life and attitudes.

Joyce Cary did something similar, on an even bigger scale, in his story of several overlapping lives in three novels, *Herself Surprised*, related by Sarah Monday, Jimson's wife, *To Be a Pilgrim*, related by Henry Wilcher, Sarah's employer, and *The Horse's Mouth*, related by Gulley Jimson himself, a sincere, dedicated painter who is in most other respects a selfish scamp. In each novel Cary impersonates one character and sees only as much of the situations as that person sees, relating it in an appropriate style.

A novelist may also use multiple impersonation of minor characters, with different purpose. Emily Brontë begins *Wuthering Heights* by allowing Mr Lockwood, an unsociable and priggish, but inoffensive, man, to describe his first encounter with Heathcliff and the dead Cathy. He then invites Nelly Dean, housekeeper at Thrushcross Grange, to tell him something of the neighbours; for twenty-six out of thirty chapters she unfolds the story, then Mr Lockwood resumes; then Nelly tells the rest of the story. Nelly's own character comes out in her narrative: she is a sane, solid countrywoman with good practical sense and good intentions, but unable to deal with the violent passions among which she finds herself, or to see anything in them beyond wilfulness and wickedness. The story takes an added sadness from the inadequacy of the most self-controlled and sensible person, and her often angry bewilderment increases the sense of awe before the anarchic emotions. The obvious weakness is that such a woman could hardly have produced such a coherent, economical and proportioned narrative; Emily Brontë evidently feels this difficulty, for she makes Nelly explain how she has done a good deal of thinking and reading. The point of view changes when Nelly reads aloud a long letter from Isabella Linton; but the solid personality of Nelly helps to give credibility to the improbable story.

Wilkie Collins in *The Moonstone* tells the first half of the story as from the pen of Gabriel Betteredge, House-Steward in the service of Lady Verinder, an elderly man with a great fondness for *Robinson Crusoe*. The second half is told by Miss Clack, a comic puritanical fanatic, who imagines herself 'a Christian persecuted by the world'; then Matthew Bruff, a sensible lawyer; Franklin Blake, the pleasant hero of the tale; Ezra Jennings, a doctor's assistant, Franklin Blake again; Sergeant Cuff, the detective; Mr Candy, a doctor; then Mr Betteredge again; with a prologue from a 'family paper' and an epilogue from 'Sergeant Cuff's man', a ship's captain and an explorer.

Kingsley Amis, in *Take a Girl Like You*, tells most of the story from the point of view of the young teacher, Jenny Bunn, following many of her naïve though amiable thoughts as well as her actions and sense-impressions; but he also sometimes follows her boy-friend Patrick Standish, super-ficially more sophisticated, also more selfish; so that we can watch the development of the pathetically inadequate relationship between two immature but not unlikeable people; this double impersonation (in the third person) shows us, much better than moralizing would, how far the two really are from one another, and from any of the awareness or considerateness of deep love.

Modern examples of the relatively rare impersonal approach, neither identifying with a character nor comment-ing upon it, are John Hersey's *The Child Buyer*, in which the whole story is told in the form of a transcript of a hearing before an American State Senate Standing Committee, with each witness and each senator speaking in character; and the novels of Ivy Compton-Burnett, which consist almost entirely of very stylized and formal dialogue; her plots are sensational, the tone calm and restrained. Characters are intensely scrupulous about the meanings of words, and much of the dialogue consists of epigrammatic summaries of situations, emotions or principles. The technique demands strenuous reading, and is more obviously artificial than the conventions of most novels; but it can be very impressive.

In *Hard Times* Dickens is throughout an omniscient narrator, watching all his characters from a distance, focusing now on one, now on another, but never really looking through the eyes of one. Reading *Hard Times* rather resembles seeing a film: the producer cuts from one scene to another, choosing incidents that show something characteristic or significant; he shows what he needs, then cuts to something else. The nearest he comes to following someone is during Mrs Sparsit's pursuit of Louisa, but he identifies with neither. This standing back from the subject allows some comic exaggeration and some commentary.

George Eliot in *Silas Marner* also writes as an omniscient

narrator, but tends to come closer to her characters than Dickens. The reader may like to observe how in the course of the novel she varies the exact point of view, sometimes focusing closely on Silas, Godfrey or, once, Nancy, sometimes standing back to give a broader picture.

In *The Europeans*, an early work, Henry James does keep to that 'muffled majesty of irresponsible authorship' he later deplored; he writes as an omniscient narrator who now and then focuses on the thoughts of one particular person. It begins very impersonally, as though offering a general description rather than a scene-setting statement. The first close focusing on a person is on Eugenia when she goes out, then later on Gertrude alone in the house. The author moves from one character to another for fairly short spells; and the last few lines of the book suddenly spread into a statement so general and large-scale as to seem ironically flat: a summary of the matrimonial combinations, with Acton's wife not even named, and a telling omission of any explanation of what happened to Eugenia. James never invites us to identify ourselves with one of the characters.

Anna of the Five Towns is told throughout by an omniscient narrator, but is very much the story of one person, Anna Tellwright, and Bennett follows her closely for much of the story. When not following Anna, he is often giving a general picture of life in the Potteries: a pot-bank, the activities of a Wesleyan chapel, and so on. The novel combines a very broad social study of the Potteries as they were at the turn of the century with a concentrated study of one good woman's tragedy. Most of the other characters are real enough, but made so with a few telling strokes apiece; the only other person Bennett follows anywhere is Anna's oppressive father, at the beginning of Chapter 9, where there is some explanation of his habitually disagreeable behaviour.

The Secret Agent is very much a novel of the omniscient narrator, and openly expresses Conrad's loathing of fatuous and callous terrorism. The tone is one of angry irony combined with compassion for the victims; the effects are gained rather by what may be described as a very fine imitation of objectivity, than by following individuals. The reader may like to verify how Conrad presents the characters in some detail, but gives the impression of a scientist at a microscope: he shifts the angle of vision from time to time, but does not follow any character with warm sympathy, except perhaps when Mrs Verloc's mother enters the almshouse, or occasionally when Winnie is suffering. Worth close study is the eleventh chapter where Conrad flashes an intense light first on Winnie, then on her husband, alternately, showing how neither is taking in the other's state of mind. Conrad's novel derives some of its haunting power from its drastic shifts of points of view: through most of the story, the narrator is an ironical, cool, contemptuous observer; at a crisis he goes close to the characters and magnifies writhing specimens under a lens. The ugly absurdities and callousnesses of terrorism, psychopathic playing at politics, and the professional coolness of police work, are the background; then we see the detailed horror of individual suffering, and how the wicked stupidity of others makes sacrifice vain and turns a generous, unselfish woman into a murderer. This sudden narrowing of focus makes the point of the book: political action is not manipulating puppets, but affecting live, complex human beings.

4

PLOT

'This blessed plot. . . .'

Shakespeare: *Richard II*, Act II, Scene 1

The plot is important to a novel much as the skeleton is important to a human body; it is simple compared with some other systems, but it gives the organism its structure and holds it together.

A plot is a story, a selection of events arranged in time, and one reason why we go on reading a novel is to see what happens next. A true plot, however, is rather more; it has causality; one thing leads to another; and another reason why we go on reading a novel is that we are interested in why things happen. A plot has a beginning which leads through a middle to an end; it makes some kind of pattern; the probability must appear not only in events, but in their sequence; a plot contains motives, consequences, relationships.

Here is a story outline:

'A bad man married a rich young woman for her money. They had a son. The man ill-treated the wife, but was eventually killed in an accident. After a time the widow married a good man. They lived a useful happy life and had two children. The son of the first marriage gave trouble, but later improved and became a social worker.'

Though love and parenthood and death are among the major concerns of human life, and this story tells of important events, it is uninteresting. Now let us turn the story into a real plot, in which there are some reasons for events:

'Laura, left at twenty heiress to a fortune, was charming

45

and affectionate, but had been over-protected by her parents, knew little of the world, and had a longing for romance. Claude, a cynical youth with good looks and a flattering tongue, made her infatuated with him, though Peter, a young doctor, was among the friends and relatives who tried to open Laura's eyes to Claude's insincerity. Her own sweet nature led her to trust him, and they were married. Claude, who wanted only her money, took her to a backward corner of Europe, where the customary subordination of woman made his tyranny easier. By the time their son was born, Laura had realized her mistake; and her husband proved also to be brutally jealous, not from love but from ugly possessiveness. He even drove her spaniel out of the house. One day, after a dispute, he locked Laura into the cold scullery. The dog was bitten by a rabid stray, sought its home again, and attacked Claude; when he screamed for help, Laura could not get out; he died from hydrophobia. When Laura, back in England, had recovered her health, she understood Peter's worth, and they were married. Her harsh experiences had made her the more appreciative of kindness and loyalty, and she became a good wife. They had a son and a daughter. Laura's son by Claude, with bad heredity and childhood insecurity, became a problem, wilful and selfish, but life in a peaceful household helped him to mature. One day, when Peter called on his help in an emergency, he learned the satisfaction of helping others; he eventually became a probation officer who brought great understanding to his work, and the good looks he had inherited from his father were an advantage to him for innocent purposes.'

This is a pretty bad plot; melodramatic, imitative and sentimental; but it is a plot, not just a story; there is a rudimentary sense of motive and consequence; people learn by experience; the events form a pattern. A good novelist who took over such a plot (perhaps for a bet!) might even make something quite good of it by subtle handling.

Plot

In mainstream novels the plot is the vital framework. It satisfies our primitive, simple interest in what happens next; it provides enjoyable suspense, excitement and surprise. If we ask any non-academic reader what a novel he has read was about, he is likely to summarize the plot for us.

Perhaps plot is not quite so important as we are apt to think: part of its function may be not only to keep the reader interested, but to keep the writer to a clear route. The plot provides structure, organizes the novel; but does even an experienced reader ever take in a novel as a whole? We can seldom see any work of art all in proportion and all intensely, any more than we can see some political problem or family situation. How many of the people who genuinely enjoy music really experience a symphony fully, in all its detail and as a whole? How many sincere lovers of painting have a total experience of a complex picture such as Crivelli's *Annunciation*, Dürer's *Nativity*, Rubens's *Judgment of Paris* or Picasso's *Guernica*? This imperfection in our response is of course one reason why it is worth while to read a book, hear a symphony, or gaze at a painting more than once; but we may never exhaust it.

We do not take in the whole plot of a novel at a first reading, still less some of the more subtle causal relationships; yet one function of the plot is to carry us forward, even though we do not grasp every detail.

We enjoy suspense; but for real suspense there must be causality. If a man in a thriller is tied to a chair with a bomb-fuse lighted on the table and a cobra on the floor, we know certain possibilities: he may free himself, his captor or someone else may free him; otherwise, the snake may bite him, or not; the bomb may explode, or not, and so on; our interest is in which possible alternative will occur. But if he is imprisoned in a room with cheese walls, from which turtles and sticks of rhubarb pop out at intervals, he hears music in a twelve-tone scale coming out of soap teacups, he is tied up with spun sugar which he cannot break, the room is lit by burning icicles standing in candlesticks carved out of liver . . . real suspense is no longer possible; there are no probabilities. If we have no notion of what may happen next, we cannot have an interesting choice. This is one reason why we want some verisimilitude in even the most sensational or fantastic escapist fiction.

Besides carrying us forward by keeping us in suspense, a plot lets us follow the workings of causality; we may go forwards and see what leads to what, or backwards and find out why. We watch how consequences follow acts; how people learn by experience; how there are rewards, punishments, vengeance, forgiveness, reconciliation, misunderstanding and clarification, reactions of people to events, creating of events by people, fresh reactions and further events. To the mature, attentive reader this demonstration of laws of life is more interesting even than suspense and excitement; but we probably need a fairly substantial—and enquiring—experience of life before we fully enjoy this aspect of a novel.

Another function of a plot is simply to provide pegs or shelving where the author can put things that he wishes to display. His chief interest may be in character and motive; but characters reveal themselves in action. He may want to explore a moral problem: how far may we manipulate other people, even with good intentions (part of the theme of E. M. Forster's *Where Angels Fear to Tread*); whether a usually wrong action may be justified in a special case (*Heart of Midlothian*); how far an artist has the right to repudiate other responsibilities for the sake of his art (Joyce Cary's *The Horse's Mouth*; Somerset Maugham's *The Moon and Sixpence*); but dilemmas do not float in the air; a moral problem means nothing until it is attached to persons in a situation.

The author's main purpose may be to expose some evil,

Plot

to make a protest, as in Walter Greenwood's *Love on the Dole* (destructive effects of unemployment and poverty) or Arthur Koestler's *Darkness at Noon* (in particular, Stalinist repression, but also the warping of the moral sense once we accept any doctrine so uncritically as to convince ourselves that the end justifies the means); a tale about the victims of such evils will affect more readers than a tract. The author may want to give a picture of some condition of society: a picture of landless, exploited farm workers in John Steinbeck's *The Grapes of Wrath*; of the collectivization of Soviet agriculture in Mikhail Sholokhov's *Virgin Soil Upturned*; of a public school in Alec Waugh's *The Loom of Youth*. He may just wish to make us laugh (the main function of the stories of P. G. Wodehouse); but if any of these purposes are to be served in fictional form, there must be a plot.

Plot in itself is at its most important in tales intended as mere entertainment: detective and crime stories, thrillers, Westerns, light romances, the lighter science fiction, adventure stories, and so on.

A good example of a suspense story of almost undiluted plot is *Flight into Danger*, by John Castle and Arthur Hailey. It is well calculated to distract a tired reader for a couple of hours. It gives vicarious excitement with reasonable probability, a background well sketched and a touch of the moral exaltation we feel when we read of people battling bravely against heavy odds. A charter flight from Winnipeg to Vancouver goes normally until a woman is taken ill. Several others follow; a doctor diagnoses dangerous food poisoning; weather conditions make an unscheduled landing impossible. Down in Vancouver, airport officials start emergency procedures; then both pilots are incapacitated. The only hope is that an ex-airforce pilot, who has never flown anything bigger than a fighter plane and that thirteen years before, may be able to bring the aircraft down safely under guidance. A suitable captain, Treleaven, sets out to teach this

49

man, Spencer, fast, by radio, how to control the huge aircraft, with one stewardess to help him. The remainder of the book is an account, mostly in dialogue and with many technicalities, of how Treleaven talks Spencer down, with passengers panicking, reporters adding to the tension in the airport, trouble with the radio, time running out for the sick, and, of course, Spencer's own nerves a factor in the problem. He manages an inelegant but safe landing. The story is marvellously handled. It made me thirsty and accelerated my pulse; it must be near the top of the class of suspense stories. But in the whole world of fiction that contains, say, *Middlemarch, Emma, Nostromo, Sons and Lovers, The Golden Bowl* and *Ulysses*, it is nowhere, because the brilliant plot is very nearly *all* it contains.

It may be compared with another novel of suspense, in which again technical detail both gives the authenticity and is important in the plot: C. S. Forester's *The Good Shepherd*, a novel about a United States Navy convoy across the Atlantic during the Second World War, and its commander, George Krause. Most of the story is told in orders from the bridge and the responses. This book is ultimately of more literary worth than *Flight into Danger*, for several reasons: the character of Krause is portrayed in more detail than that of Spencer; the wider significance of the job being done—in the struggle for comparative freedom against totalitarianism—is kept in mind and there is a sense of purpose and historical perspective; we see more complexity of human motives, more differentiation of character; the decisions are more complex and involve difficult moral questions that have to be solved fast, with problems of discipline, professional etiquette, technological and tactical possibilities, psychological factors. The story is exciting, full of plot twists, suspense, action; it is also a tribute to the courage, intelligence and self-discipline of the men who won the Second World War, a salutary reminder to those who have not taken part in desperate conflict of what men have done for others, and of the nobility of the true man of action; a reminder, too, of the cruelty and waste of war; it is also a novel of character, because, largely by implication and accumulation of detail, Forester gives a three-dimensional portrait of a rather rare and very valuable human type: the genuine, unselfish leader of men, who subordinates his own desires to a great purpose, yet considers the needs of other individuals. Krause is many times aware of selfish concerns, yet pushes them into second place. He is vulnerable; his religion is a source of strength, yet also of neurotic guilt; he lives with bitter career disappointment and a tragic failure in marriage; the body he forces to slogging endurance has the crying needs common to all.

Similarly, the detective tale we remember or re-read is the one in which plot is combined with some roundness in some of the characters, some depth in the examination of motive, or some vitality in the background. Conan Doyle's stories are old-fashioned now, but Holmes and Watson live. In 1971 a friend, irritated by my slowness on the uptake, exclaimed, 'Heavens, even Dr Watson would have seen that!' Hercule Poirot, Lord Peter Wimsey, Father Brown, Inspector Ghote, are not comparable with Dorothea Casaubon, Captain Ahab, Becky Sharp or Anna Karenina; but they do have their own life, though it is more a life of traits and mannerisms than of human totality; and they bring the light detective story nearer to the true novel. Simenon's Maigret is another matter; many of the Maigret stories might be classed as true novels.

A good detective story in one sense needs a 'better' plot than a major novel of character, in that the principle of 'fair play' (giving the reader all the clues the detective has) necessitates the closest attention to details and consistency.

Techniques of plotting vary. On the whole a novel could be slower-moving before the advent of competing forms of entertainment such as cinema, radio and television.

Richardson and Fielding could digress and sermonize; and in all early fiction there was more use for long descriptions of physical appearance, scenery, costume; there is little point now in spending pages on presenting a visual image that television can present in seconds. In an era in which all educated Englishmen had a classical education, Fielding could in *Tom Jones* make an elaborate joke of imitating Homeric epic; this part of what is still a grand novel now falls flat with many readers. We now expect either faster-moving plots, or experimental novels in which plot is unimportant.

Victorian novels were often published in three volumes, so the plot sometimes showed signs of division into thirds. Novels were fairly expensive, and many readers obtained them by subscribing to circulating libraries. These, in the Victorian era, exercised a good deal of unofficial censorship (as a chain of bookstores may do today), and this somewhat restricted an author in his choice of plot or treatment of a subject, especially one with a sexual element.

Plot construction was in Victorian times affected by the common practice of publishing full-length novels in serial form in magazines, or in monthly parts. Novels that first appeared in parts include *Dombey and Son*, *Nicholas Nickleby*, *David Copperfield*, *Bleak House* and *Little Dorrit*; *Vanity Fair* and *Pendennis*; *Middlemarch* and *Daniel Deronda*; Disraeli's first novel, *Vivian Grey* and Trollope's *Can You Forgive Her?* Novels that first appeared as serials in magazines include Wilkie Collins's *The Woman in White* and Mrs Gaskell's *Cranford* (in *Household Words*, edited by Dickens); George Eliot's *Romola*, Mrs Gaskell's *Wives and Daughters* and Meredith's *Harry Richmond* (in the *Cornhill Magazine*); *Great Expectations* (in *All the Year Round*); Charles Kingsley's *Hypatia* and *Yeast* (in *Fraser's Magazine*); Henry James's *Roderick Hudson* (in the *Atlantic Monthly*) and Meredith's *Evan Harrington* (in the *Fortnightly Review*).

This practice of serial publication had several effects on

structure. Sales are promoted if each instalment of a serial ends with an interesting question unanswered—a startling statement, alarming predicament, crucial dilemma. Even if an instalment does not end leaving us in suspense, it has to have an end; it needs some kind of unity. Some of the melodramatic effects in Dickens's plots sprang from the requirements of serial publication. These may also have had much to do with the popularity of plots involving deceits, disguises, missing people, unmaskings, surprises and reunions. Serial publication makes it almost obligatory for a plot to include numerous climaxes, a shape that might be represented something like this:

whereas the plot of a non-serial novel could if so desired be more like this:

Of course suspense has its function in most plots of novels; but serial publication tends to increase its importance and require climaxes timed for reasons that are not artistic.

It also had the effect of inviting what fashionable jargon would call reader participation. New instalments were awaited eagerly, and readership might expand: 400 copies of the first part of *The Pickwick Papers* were printed, but 40,000 of the fifteenth! Captain Brown in *Cranford* was killed while 'deeply in perusal of a number of *Pickwick*' and in *Barchester Towers* the bishop 'read the last number of the "Little Dorrit" of the day with great inward satisfaction'. In real life, readers sometimes begged an author not to kill a character, or to let two lovers marry. Authors might have to rush instalments to meet dates; editors and publishers were alarmed if sales dropped; an author might depart from his first intention at the request of readers, or modify his plot in the hope of better sales. We know that Dickens took the advice of his friend Francis Jeffrey on an alteration of *Dombey and Son*, and that of Bulwer Lytton in changing his first intention of leaving Pip solitary at the end of *Great Expectations*; and he was uncertain about the exact plot of *David Copperfield* until he had written several numbers. Even today publishers or literary agents may advise an author to modify the first version of a novel—either for genuine artistic reasons, or with a view to better sales.

An influence on plot in the twentieth century has been the possibility of film rights, which are quite valuable. It is widely believed that many sensational modern novels have been written with one eye on the film rights. This will induce the author to seek episodes suitable for visual presentation, perhaps something spectacular on the screen: a train crash, a large fire, a cavalry charge, a splendid ball, a massacre, a procession, an earthquake, a flood. On the other hand, a film made from a major novel is often disappointing; much that matters cannot be filmed. Attempts have been made to film *Wuthering Heights*; but that novel makes its impact by emotional sympathy, not by visual images. I once saw a film of the lesser novel *Lorna Doone* which seemed utterly commonplace; the novel is certainly better than commonplace. How could anyone make a film of *Middlemarch* or *The Egoist* or *The Ambassadors* or *To the Lighthouse* that was not a travesty? The hope that a novel may appear dramatized on television may have some effect on plot construction, though the dramatization may, as on the bigger screen, be disappointing.

A modern novelist is not to blame if in devising a plot for a novel he has a quarter of an eye on film or television possibilities; he is at fault only if he writes a bad novel and does not mind its becoming a bad film. The perfect writer would presumably be one whose motive was 100 per cent artistic, who was indifferent to material gain, the pleasures of success, the humiliations of failure; who would revise and polish his work for years, a man of vocation as single-hearted as a saint. Anyone trying to write anything, even for the school magazine, ought to have some such ideal in mind; but such a dedication, like all moral ideals, is more easily formulated than practised! Writers have the same needs and the same liabilities to personal obligations as other people. Most writers have either to earn a living in some other occupation or to pay considerable attention to questions of sales. Though having to work for a living is not itself a grievance, the seriously intending writer who has to hold another job to support himself or his family is thereby condemned to do what for him amounts to wasting the greater part of his time and energy; whereas the full-time writer, having to think about saleability, may have much self-reproach and anxiety as to the enforced insincerities. Except for a very few, writing is a very ill-paid occupation, very precarious, and without adequate superannuation arrangements. It is, as are all the creative arts, also a profession in which one may never receive any payment for months of work. A novelist can hardly be expected to take no thought at all for his bread and butter.

Even questions of production economics may affect plot; a publisher may ask for a book to be made longer or shorter, not as a matter of aesthetics or censorship, but to suit sales prospects and production costing! He may want a book to fit a series. This all seems absurd; but creative genius may be loosed in odd ways: *The Pickwick Papers*, which set Dickens on the road to fame, developed out of a publisher's request to write some text for a set of drawings.

There are fashions in plot as in other things; and in studying literature we should try not to be swayed by mere fashion. Nothing is easier than to advertise our sophistication by clever sneers at something uncongenial to a temporary climate of opinion; and it is easier to imitate some respected critic by copying his style of dismissal than by attentively following his subtle analysis of his favourite novels.

The Victorians liked a well constructed, well defined plot structure, with marked turns of fortune, surprises, discoveries. Another favoured early theme is that of a journey or a quest, as in *Joseph Andrews* or *Heart of Midlothian*. There was a preference for a plot that was worked out to a conclusion, such as a marriage or marriages, the righting of a wrong, the defeat of a villain; often the novelist tied up any loose ends in the final paragraphs. Until recently there was a convention of the 'happy ending'; the good achieved their wishes and the wicked were thwarted.

Yet one of the central mysteries of life strikes us at an early age, and leads the reader to some critical doubts over the conventional 'happy ending'; we see that the good, harmless and lovable often suffer severely, not only from accident, illness or bereavement, but from such misfortunes as we would like to think goodness and wisdom could avert: career disasters, unhappy marriage, treachery of friends, public disgrace, disappointed parenthood. We often see the selfish and malicious prosper. We see how selfish and vicious people are often pleased with themselves, often boastfully complacent (like Mr Bounderby), while harmless kindly people who try to do right may ache daily with guilty consciences. We can scorn the 'happy ending' too cynically; when all fairytale morality has been abandoned, it is still true that intelligent helpfulness, honest effort, integrity, patience, balance, sane and generous love, constructive purposes, perseverance, courage, tact, tolerance, courtesy, self-discipline and other virtues are at least more likely to contribute to a fairly happy life than are greed, rudeness, bullying, gross selfishness, laziness, hatred, envy, touchiness, self-importance, unbridled self-indulgence, cowardice and other failings. Granted moderate health and spared catastrophic bad luck, Adam

Bede and Jane Eyre, Jeanie Deans and Felix Holt, would most probably enjoy more happiness and even popularity and prosperity than Hetty Sorrel or Mrs Reed, George Staunton or Mr Jermyn.

Today we also question more openly the conventional assumptions that the marriage of two people who love each other guarantees their happiness, or that death is the ultimate catastrophe. We admit that promising marriages may go wrong; most of us fear something such as paralysis or destitution more than death.

Indeed, literature reflects an odd ambiguity in our attitude to death. Several religions teach that death may be only the gateway to fuller life—at least for some people; and, though the belief in immortality is no longer an obligation of respectability, psychical research keeps the subject open. Yet the serious treatment in fiction of death as a possibility of joy and adventure is rare, and some attempts at handling it thus, such as the death of Little Nell in *The Old Curiosity Shop*, or of Tom in *Uncle Tom's Cabin*, displease modern readers as sentimental. Perhaps we do not read them aright. Romain Rolland at the end of *Jean-Christophe* tries a more sophisticated suggestion of death as a gate to life; Charles Williams in *All Hallows' Eve* and *Descent into Hell* writes seriously of life after death. (Ghost stories, a common form of sensational entertainment, rarely carry serious implications about human souls.) We often find in novels contradictory attitudes to death that are realistic imitations of real life; how does Mr Casaubon, a clergyman, so committed to Christian belief, manage to make a mean, spiteful codicil to his will when he knows he may die of heart disease at any moment—but who finds it incredible?

The conventional 'happy ending' is now almost confined to more or less escapist reading; the convention of tying up loose ends is forgotten. Thomas Hardy specialized in the sad and unfair ending. If we are to accept a happy ending today, it must be more provisional: the hero has not solved all the problems, but has sorted some things out and moved in a promising direction. Both Bernard Malamud's *A New Life* and John Wain's *A Winter in the Hills* are stories of redemption through caring for others and accepting responsibility. In each the hero reaches a point where he has developed considerably, put some past mistakes behind him, and is about to marry the heroine; but it will be after the humiliations of divorce; he will have weighty problems, including stepchildren; and he has also suffered some defeat and wasted effort. In Wain's novel we see at the end the prospective stepchildren being innocent boring little pests, and their truth to life makes such happiness as there is more convincing.

Often twentieth-century novels do not even have what a Victorian reader would think of as an ending; the neat, implausibly symmetrical plot is a thing of the past in the serious novel; life goes on.

There are also changes in the subject-matter. We can soon dismiss the obvious changes brought about by technological and organizational developments. A modern Jeanie Deans could start a press campaign; or could hitch-hike to London in a day or two; Gerard the son of Eli could telephone Sevenbergen from Rome; a course of tranquillizers might have helped Marianne Dashwood. Today death in childbed is rare, but road accidents are common. Plots depending on disguises, deceptions as to identity or parenthood, disappearances and abductions, are not easily made plausible, except in historical novels, because of modern police methods and such matters as National Insurance cards, the electoral roll and the rating authorities. There are no little local banks to break and wipe out the fortunes of innocent people. The welfare services, for all their imperfections, have removed many agonies of the days of Hardy or even Gissing. A single woman without an unearned income need not become a governess, domestic drudge or kept mistress; she may, if she is able and hard-working, hope to become a professor, a cabinet minister, a QC, a doctor; or, if less gifted, earn good money in one of a large variety of jobs. Huge families are now rare. For three generations to live under one roof is felt as a misfortune. Domestic service as found in novels until about the Second World War is now virtually non-existent.

There are more subtle changes. Partly because of the rise of psychoanalysis, serious novelists today are much more aware of symbolism and more interested in the unconscious mind and hidden motives. New insights into psychology and sociology can make a novelist more charitable and sensitive, or merely sophisticated and cynical. The liberalization of sexual mores has made many assumptions of Victorian plots impossible today; an adulterer may now be a sympathetic character; illegitimacy has lost its shock value; a woman who has had a love-affair is not 'ruined' and a man and woman are not 'compromised' injuriously by being alone together; homosexuality is not only possible as a subject, but even open to sympathetic treatment; forced marriages for money, or parental authority as brutal as that of Squire Western in *Tom Jones*, are out of the question.

Mrs Craik's *John Halifax, Gentleman* (1857) could not be written today. Richard Hughes's *A High Wind in Jamaica* could not have been written much before 1918. Both are novels of some merit.

John Halifax, Gentleman tells how a penniless lad achieves prosperity, dignity and happy marriage chiefly by hard work, sensible initiative and good conduct. Through the novel runs a rather over-simplified, though not silly, morality, and Christian beliefs that today seem naïvely literal. The ultimate happy ending is the death of John and his wife with the implication that they will now be happy together in a better world—a Christian logic greater novelists have seldom followed so completely. John's desire to be a 'gentleman' is not snobbery; he wants to prosper, but has high ideals of gentlemanly conduct. It is not wholly to our credit that the sophisticated reader of today can hardly take the novel seriously and may be tempted to read bits of it in a guying manner. The price of our deeper insights into human complexities has for some been a defeatism and negativism no wiser than Mrs Craik's naïve decencies. Our emphasis on democracy may be a matter of vinegary envy as easily as of generous brotherhood; we can now be too suspicious of deserved success, too hostile to reasonable authority, too reluctant to grant that some values, even some people, are worth more than others. If we can summon up enough historical sense to stop sniggering at the unfashionable moral tone, we may find parts of the novel touching, and even enjoy some strokes of dry humour:

> 'I'm a person of independent property, which consists of my head and two hands, out of which I hope to realize a large capital some day.'. . .
> 'Our neighbours may think of us exactly what they like. Half the sting of poverty is gone when one keeps house for one's own comfort, and not for the comments of one's neighbours.'

Yet such a novel, turning on self-help and rather literalistic evangelistic piety, is impossible today; any specifically Christian novel will be more like the best work of Graham Greene.

A High Wind in Jamaica treats of an aspect of experience with which Victorian novelists did not deal in detail: children, seen not as miniature adults, but as creatures living a far more alien life, in an innocent but total self-centredness and with very little comprehension or even awareness of anyone else. The plot framework is sensational: an English couple in Jamaica, after an earthquake and hurricane, send their children, with two others, to England. The ship is captured by pirates. One little boy dies in a genuine accident; the adolescent girl is raped with serious effects on her mind; the other children have, in their own way, a rather happy time. When the pirates are captured, the ringleaders are condemned to death largely on the evidence of the child, Emily, who in fact in a panic committed the murder herself. She does not understand what she has done and is more interested in the fate of the family cat. The brilliance and originality of the novel lie in the study of the real horror of non-communication, and the macabre relationship of the fantasy worlds of the children to the grim realities of adult conflicts. The sufferings of the older girl are seen through the uncomprehending, unpitying eyes of the younger children. The story is full of dreadful ironies, grim humour and shrewd observation of children; it would have been impossible before the development of child psychology and a revulsion from sentimental portrayals of children in fiction.

Subject-matter varies; but all plots have some relationship to Time, because cause and effect take place in Time. (The egg may have been thrown at the wall for one of several reasons: accident, spite, mistake, anger, or even joke; but not because it is now trickling down the wall.)

The most obvious treatment of Time, and the commonest and probably easiest to read, is to tell the story in the order in which the events happened. Often the novelist may tell two or more stories, alternating them, but in natural time-sequence, until events link two or more parallel stories into one stream. In *Romola*, for instance, the stories of Tito's marriage to Romola and his relationship to the deluded Tessa are told separately until in the fifteenth chapter Romola accidentally meets Tessa; only in the fifty-sixth chapter does she begin to grasp the situation.

The *flashback* is common: some of the story is related in the obvious time-sequence, but part is narrated by one of the characters, or in some document or letter, and this explains what has gone before. In *Pride and Prejudice* a long letter from

Plot

Darcy shows the attractive Wickham in a new light, and, by revealing a portion of the past, greatly affects the future. A flashback somewhere is almost inevitable in any novel in which a mystery is revealed: Wilkie Collins's *The Moonstone*, Dickens's *A Tale of Two Cities*, Scott's *The Antiquary* or even Henry James's *Portrait of a Lady*. Flashbacks may also be used to give variety, or to let a character reveal himself by telling something from his own point of view.

Novelists have experimented with other ways of treating time: *Tristram Shandy* is the first English novel to distort the time-sequence out of all rational order. Less drastic are scenes of reminiscence, or of groping efforts to recollect, or the comedy or irony of someone's distortion of a story the reader already knows. An enquiry into past events is the normal form of the detective story. Charles Reade's *Griffith Gaunt* begins:

'Then I say once for all, that priest shall never darken my doors again.'

'Then I say they are my doors and not yours, and that holy man shall brighten them whenever he will.'

The gentleman and lady, who faced each other, pale and furious, and interchanged this bitter defiance, were man and wife. And had loved each other well.

Reade then tells the story leading up to this state of affairs, reaching this crisis once again in the middle of the twentieth chapter; the rest of the novel describes the developments after the crisis. In Anne Brontë's *The Tenant of Wildfell Hall* the first fifteen chapters present a mysterious young woman, seen through the eyes of Gilbert Markham; at the end of the fifteenth chapter she gives him her diary of the previous six years—giving an enormous flashback taking twenty-eight chapters—before Markham resumes his story. The last part of the story is told in letters from the lady.

The extent of time may range from a lifetime, as in Romain

Plot

Rolland's *Jean-Christophe*, to a few seconds, as in William Golding's *Pincher Martin*. Most mainstream novels cover either some years in the lives of a group of people (*Middlemarch, Villette, Great Expectations, Tess of the D'Urbervilles*) or some days or weeks (Stephen Crane's *The Red Badge of Courage*, Herman Melville's *Moby Dick*, William Golding's *The Spire* or *The Inheritors*). *Mrs Dalloway, Ulysses* and *One Day in the Life of Ivan Denisovich* each cover a single day. Where the real time covered is very short, there will be something in addition to the day's direct experience: memories, flashbacks, fantasies, explanations—some devices to create sequences of cause and effect, or relationships, to make a kind of plot.

The plot of a novel may be so simple that it can be summarized in a few lines, or so complex that it is almost beyond summarizing. *Riceyman Steps* and *The Secret Agent* gain some of their laser-like intensity from the simplicity of plot and small cast; *War and Peace* derives some of its power from the panoramic plot that gives us a sense of seeing the impact of history upon individuals.

We may have a simple plot with a single story, like *Riceyman Steps*; *Jane Eyre* or *Moll Flanders*, with more events, are still basically simple plots, each treating of one person's experiences; Henry James's *The Golden Bowl* and *The Wings of the Dove* are simple in plot, though they are subtle and complex novels in their study of thought, motive and character. In a complex plot we follow the experiences of several characters and several sequences of events, linked with some skill and regard for probability. Examples include: *Quentin Durward, Bleak House, Daniel Deronda, Pendennis*, Mrs Gaskell's *Wives and Daughters, The Story of an African Farm*, Hardy's *The Return of the Native*, Steinbeck's *East of Eden*, Mary McCarthy's *The Group*, Dostoievski's *The Brothers Karamazov* and *Crime and Punishment*, Manzoni's *The Betrothed*; the reader can think of other examples.

In some novels we find an unmistakable principal plot

with a sub-plot or sub-plots of less importance; this is not the same as a complex plot in which all the threads are of about equal thickness. The little love story of Dick Swiveller and the servant is a minor sub-plot in *The Old Curiosity Shop*; there may be minor incidents which do not move the action forward (though they often throw light on character): there are many, often practical jokes, in Smollett's novels: the incident in *The Vicar of Wakefield* when Moses Primrose is sent to sell a horse and returns with a gross of green spectacles is an example from Goldsmith. Charles Lever's *Charles O'Malley* has entertaining, almost self-contained episodes rather than real plot development.

A good plot suits the characters, tone and background of a novel. Unlikely, farcical events will go better with hilariously eccentric characters, as in *Humphry Clinker*, than with characters studied in depth with psychological realism. We may be more ready to believe in strange motives if the setting is exotic, but the plot must be credible at least in its setting, even in frank fantasy. A strange world in science fiction must at least have some sort of consistency; and character should somewhat affect plot, as in H. G. Wells's *The First Men in the Moon* and *Men Like Gods*. Even invented non-humans, such as C. S. Lewis's Marsh-wiggle or Tolkien's hobbits, need some sort of self-consistent psychology.

All plots are extremely simple in comparison with the complexities of real life; even *Ulysses*, which seems like an all-inclusive study of a day, has more pattern and coherence than real life; it is still a literary creation imposing order upon chaos. The mainstream novel concerns itself with situations that are in some way critical; yet much of the life of even Heathcliff, Captain Ahab, Ann Veronica, Lady Chatterley, must have been spent in quiet, commonplace routines. A plot, by being thus selective, shows the sequence of cause and effect more clearly than we see it in real experience. In a novel the things that are important to us are allowed their primacy rather more than in real life. The day's work may be dismissed in a few words, even ignored: the central character racked by a dilemma does not waste half an hour looking for his other cuff-link on the floor in a bad light. Good novelists do often show or imply the pressure of irrelevancies; Jane Austen could do this with marvellous economy; but the scale is different from that of real life.

The schoolboy who after many Victorian novels asked, 'How is it that in books people never go to the lavatory?' had a genuine question, though he might have grown sick of Swift's or Smollett's mention of the subject; most of us can think of impossibly uninterrupted conversations or incidents in novels. Yet the omission is not merely squeamish; it is part of the general omission of irrelevant routines we take for granted.

The writer's own ideology will affect his choice of plot: George Gissing gave great emphasis to money, because he felt so fiercely the importance of the economic factor in life; D. H. Lawrence's plots are always in some way concerned with sincerity and depth in human relationships. One writer might see a terrorist as just destructive and evil, another as a patriotic martyr; a greater novelist might be more interested in motivation and the tragic ambiguity of the man's moral position. An African nationalist would scarcely create a plot implying good faith and skill in a colonial civil servant, any more than a writer of strong imperialist convictions would make an honest African nationalist his hero. But the *merely* ideological novel can hardly be great literature; the best of us must, in our human finiteness, have some prejudices and failures of understanding; but the greatest novelists are distinguished by, among other things, superior breadth of mind, ability to see many points of view and enter into many kinds of experience, and a sensitive awareness of complexity, ambiguity, paradox, confusion. This is why a great novel may increase our sympathy and charity.

Plot

The reader will find it very rewarding to examine in detail the plots of our five novels. *Hard Times* is very obvious, almost diagrammatical, in its presentation of cause and effect, with its three sections: 'Sowing', 'Reaping' and 'Garnering'. We are shown the mistakes to which Gradgrind's theory of life leads, and how experience forces him to learn. Other major themes in the plot are how falsehood may succeed for a time, but is likely to be exposed in the end; and how warm-heartedness, even without much intellectual power, may be a better guide through life than intellect without human kindness. *Hard Times*, with its ruthless chains of consequence, is one of Dickens's grimmest novels—it does not have a happy ending, or even satisfy our sense of justice—but the plot is satisfying by the strong, credible pattern, rich in bold contrasts and sharp ironies, in which the consequences work themselves out. It is a good story, full of excitement, emotion, suspense and twists; it is also a very well constructed plot.

Silas Marner is a gentler novel, but with a happier ending and a stress on redemptive experience it still emphasizes moral education and how we suffer the consequences of our mistakes. The reader who examines the plot will soon see how it fits together as neatly as a jigsaw. This is satisfying. There are few loose ends: truth is revealed, unselfish love rewarded, less perfect love chastened but not broken, deliberate wickedness punished. To modern tastes the plot may even seem a trifle too neat, too much like a puzzle with a right solution. One weakness in the pattern is that no cause is given for the childlessness of Godfrey and Nancy. The plot is perhaps brought closer to reality, rather than flawed, by the fact that Silas never has his name cleared, and no fulfilment is found for the likeable, humorous Priscilla Lammeter.

Young readers often enjoy *Silas Marner* long before they can appreciate the delicate touches of detail, the depth of insight, the dry irony or the full pathos; for the well constructed plot makes it a good tale as well as a great novel.

Plot

Few people could enjoy *The Europeans* for its story, for Henry James was not, in the usual sense, a teller of a good tale. Reading his novels, we experience them more as we experience life itself: we proceed by seeing bits of the story and picking up hints. The reader will find it much more difficult to make a detailed summary of this plot, though he may learn much by working on the novel as attentively as this demands. He will have to explain how Eugenia and Felix come to meet Mr Wentworth, Gertrude, Charlotte, Mr Brand, Lizzie and Robert Acton; how the various facts are revealed; how the two Europeans and the American group get to know one another. We are led to expect Eugenia to marry Robert, while an attempt is made to interest Clifford in Eugenia to curb his drinking; yet Eugenia refuses Robert, and it is Lizzie who becomes the wife of Clifford; the enigmatic Gertrude, awakened by Felix's love, becomes able to plead for her own happiness. Then, when the reader has sorted out all the relationships and their development, he is confronted on the last page with the almost contemptuously abrupt winding-up of the plot—without even a name given to the 'nice young girl' whom Robert married!

The Europeans was published twenty-three years before the death of Queen Victoria, but it is very unlike what we think of as a typical Victorian novel. The plot is, in a sense, unsatisfying. It seems extraordinary that we are never told what happens to Eugenia, except that she returns to Europe. Though there is much emotional development, there is hardly any incident in the usual sense; there are only conversations. Several important events take place 'off-stage' and are mentioned only in conversation; there are few explanations; the author keeps out of the picture as much as possible.

Perhaps this plot is best summarized, not by a list of apparently trivial incidents, but by its emotional content, something like this: two clever, articulate, sophisticated Europeans, not wicked, but worldly and calculating, visit the more subdued, puritanical, less lively American branch of the family, in the hope of making two prosperous matches. They cheer up the puritanical home, but it also affects them in the direction of integrity and not wanting to manipulate people; in the end they bring some happiness; Felix marries for love, though not to his financial disadvantage; Eugenia finds herself unwilling to scheme and exploit people, and departs; the Americans are reminded that though duty is important, a reasonable pursuit of happiness is also legitimate. All this is shown in a manner refined, subtle, oblique; the tone is one of understatement and emotional restraint. This is largely a new sort of novel, and James was perhaps the father of the modern experimental novel that demands more thought from the reader than the earlier mainstream novel.

Though *Anna of the Five Towns* appeared twenty-three years later, and is unmistakably more modern than George Eliot or Dickens, its plot is of the older type: there is more concrete incident, more explanation, less ambiguity. The reader will find it well worth while to try to summarize the plot and see how Bennett links the various incidents in patterns of cause and effect. This is a plot with essentially a sad ending. As often happens in real life, the good and loving suffer, the harmlessly weak perish, the ruthless and selfish tend to dominate their moral and emotional superiors. The plot is very well constructed; it provides not only credible cause and effect, but a subtle portrayal of Anna's maturing and development through her various experiences. There is surprise and even sensation, but we have been prepared by hints for the developments. This is an old-fashioned type of plot treated in a modern manner.

The Secret Agent has the simplest plot of our five books. Its ingredients are appropriate to a mere thriller: anarchists, bombs, police, murder, suicide; but they are treated with realism, emotional depth and close attention to cause and effect.

Winnie Verloc, unselfish like Anna, married Adolf Verloc without happy love, and tried to be a good wife, for the sake of Stevie, her mentally deficient brother, and her crippled mother. Verloc is a rather incompetent spy for a foreign embassy, and as an *agent provocateur* works for an anarchist group on which he reports: Michaelis, Yundt, Ossipon and the 'Professor'. The latter have no sensible plans, constructive revolutionary ideas or even humane ideals, but are wholly destructive. When we learn that a man has been blown to pieces in Greenwich Park, and that the 'Professor' made a bomb for Verloc, we suppose Verloc is the dead man. We see something of the police officer in charge, hear of an address found on the remains, and see the complications caused by the interest a lady of some standing takes in Michaelis.

Mrs Verloc's mother, to reduce the burden on the home and ensure that Stevie will be cared for, secretly arranges to enter an almshouse. Verloc spends ten days abroad, then begins, on his wife's suggestion, to take Stevie for walks. He arranges for him to visit Michaelis. Verloc plans to go abroad, but Mrs Verloc learns, in the course of a call from Inspector Heap, that it is Stevie who has been blown up. Remembering her sacrificial life, thinking of her brother's hideous death, the gentle and good woman stabs her husband to death; then thinks of suicide, then of flight; the womanizing Ossipon feigns concern, gets her to the boat train and absconds with her money. Finally we see Ossipon and the 'Professor' talking, and learn that Winnie Verloc threw herself from the cross-Channel boat. Michaelis has sunk into sloppy humanitarian fantasy; Ossipon half worships science; the 'Professor' lives on with his cult of destruction; the innocent have perished.

Though *The Secret Agent* is still a mainstream novel, with coherent plot, realistic characters and coherent style, the plotting differs from that of the other four novels in two respects.

The handling of time is more complex. The first three

chapters are in chronological order, but the death of Stevie occurs in the fourth. We do not know yet that it is Stevie; in the eighth chapter he is alive, so this is a flashback, but we are not at once aware of the fact. He is still alive when the ninth chapter begins, with Winnie confident he cannot be lost for long (because she has sewed his address into his coat); in the middle of this chapter the flashback catches up with the chronological order as Heap tells of Stevie's death. In the eleventh chapter the chronological order is broken again for flashbacks describing Verloc's relationship with Stevie, and Winnie's past. Eventually the death of Winnie is related in a newspaper cutting that has for ten days been in Ossipon's pocket. These distortions of obvious chronological order increase the sense of unravelling a mystery, and of tangles and muddle in the minds of the characters.

The other special feature of this plot is the massive irony. Winnie and her mother make sacrifices in vain—indeed, their last sacrifices for Stevie precipitate his death. Stevie is blown to bleeding gobbets *because* he cannot bear to think of people suffering; Winnie's life of devoted unselfishness creates the situation in which she murders her husband; her desperate need to trust gives Ossipon his chance to rob her of her last hope. The Assistant Commissioner hinders investigations because, for his own comfort in society, he does not want to find Michaelis guilty; but Michaelis is genuinely not guilty. The anarchists have confidence in their own importance and great ideas, while they demonstrate in word and deed their intellectual confusion, emotional and moral poverty, useless negativism, political ineptitude and essential worthlessness. All five novels have elements of irony; it is almost an inevitable ingredient in a major novel; but in *The Secret Agent* it is part of the very structure of the plot.

Plot provides the bones of these novels, of all mainstream novels; but a plot summary tells us little; character and background put meat on the bones.

5

CHARACTER

How often in the overflowing streets,
Have I gone forward with the Crowd, and said
Unto myself, the face of every one
That passes by me is a mystery.

William Wordsworth: *The Prelude* (1805 version), Book VII.

The creation of character is probably the most remarkable achievement of most great novelists. Few people can recite the plot of a novel in detail shortly after reading it; most readers of novels can remember numerous characters; we make allusions to literary characters in ordinary talk: Mr Micawber, Uriah Heep, Mr Rochester, Becky Sharp, Mr Darcy, Tess Durbeyfield, even Molly Bloom.

Character is less important in allegorical, satirical or highly experimental novels; but most major British novelists have been great creators of character: Samuel Richardson, Henry Fielding, Jane Austen, Sir Walter Scott, the Brontës, Charles Dickens, George Eliot, Anthony Trollope, Charles Reade, Thomas Hardy, Henry James, Joseph Conrad, Arnold Bennett, H. G. Wells (at his best), D. H. Lawrence, Joyce Cary; any reader of good novels can find some more names.

Creators of character do not all work the same way, and we experience fictional characters in several ways. In reading some escapist romance, we may sink into what is really an assisted daydream, identifying ourselves with hero or heroine, or possibly a colourful villain or villainess. Reading a better novel, such as *Oliver Twist* or *Jane Eyre*, we may identify ourselves with hero or heroine in a rather more intelligent, sensitive way; but this is still not the full joy of experiencing literary characters. Sometimes we need to stand back a little; we can enjoy characters we neither like nor envy, because we appreciate the vivid portrayal, the individuality. We can then relish Tom Pipes in *Peregrine Pickle*, Quilp in *The Old Curiosity Shop*, Lady Catherine de Bourgh in *Pride and Prejudice*, Paul Emmanuel in *Villette*, hungry Elsie in *Riceyman Steps*, Pinky in Graham Greene's *Brighton Rock*, Lennie in Steinbeck's *Of Mice and Men*.

We may also relish the portrayal of a character with some discomfort, when we begin, through fiction, to see ourselves in real human situations: not villains on a satisfying grand scale, but selfish, muddled, petty, full of self-deceptions; wanting to be loved but doing unlovable and love-destroying things; wanting to be good, but failing; dimly sensing that it is desirable to be balanced, rational, helpful, but slithering about in our neuroses, unreasonable expectations and varied laziness; wishing for lyrical splendours of emotion and trapped in timidity and littleness. To see, as we do in the greatest fiction, our human capacity for making mistakes, the dilemmas and perplexities, the failures to communicate, is not a wholly agreeable experience. I hope I have lived a marginally better life than Tito Melema in *Romola*, but I find it disquieting to recognize most alarming likenesses to my own inner processes in his self-justifications, choices of the immediately easier way, and slidings down the slippery incline of increasing selfishness. Literature can warn. We see, too, through fiction, the difficulties of others; it is sometimes easier to realize these through fiction than with tiresome people beside us. We are reminded that we must not generalize smugly from our small experience: Kingsley's *Alton Locke*, Lewis Grassic Gibbon's *A Scots Quair*, Zola's *L'Assommoir* or *La Terre*, show what bad social conditions can do to human character. In fiction we watch people wrestling with problems that are not our own, with choices we can be thankful we have not had to make; we see how experience educates people, often making them better, wiser, more humble before life, more perceptive; or how it may break them, making them bitter, vindictive or hopeless. All this should improve both our intelligent self-awareness and self-criticism, and our intelligent awareness of others.

The most enjoyable fictional characters seem very 'lifelike'. Sometimes this arises from vitality rather than deep psychological probability: Dickens, for instance, created many memorable characters who, on closer inspection, seem less probable; their 'characters' are mostly their mannerisms. Jane Austen's less flamboyant characters are, if we allow for social changes, more truly like the people next door.

Yet, when we compare fictional characters with the people next door, we must remember where our door is. How can a sedentary student judge the reality of Hemingway's men of action? Could a coal-miner make much sense of *The Spoils of Poynton*? Would a policeman find Bill Sykes or Fagin more or less real than a critic at his desk does? One reader may find a portrayal of a love-relationship impossibly high-flown and idealistic, while to a second reader what the first reader sees as a truer picture is a mere encounter of animal natures with nothing of what he calls love; both presentations, and both judgments, could be based on well observed experience.

We do not know the people we meet in real life; we do not know ourselves; we must constantly try to love, or live at peace with, people we do not understand, to accept their otherness, to grasp that we are as alien and as puzzling to them, to remember that each person is the centre of his or her own universe. Reading good novels is one way of enlarging our understanding; so we should not too hastily dismiss something as impossible.

Moreover, just as we cannot in real life fully understand another human being, we cannot expect even the greatest novelist to give a total portrait of a complete person. Characters may be important in novels at different levels, just as people are important to us at different levels in real life. The life with no deep relationships is tragically trivial and stunted: most people aim at a close understanding with a spouse, close family, and a few intimate friends; but we can also be on 'friendly' terms with a great many people—scores, even hundreds—to whom we feel some selective goodwill; we do them small kindnesses, we like their company. We also meet shop assistants, bus conductors, traffic wardens, postmen, waitresses, dustmen, doctors, meter readers, into whose characters we have no insight at all and whom we notice only as doing a job well or badly, being pleasant or disagreeable. Our idea of good relations with them is for both parties to be civil and co-operative. Similarly a novelist will try to portray some characters in depth; will have some identified by a few mannerisms; will see some from one angle only. The chief characters probably meet some people who rate only a few sentences: the servant who says my lady is not at home, the messenger who delivers the vital telegram, the driver of the coach, the doctor whose one task is to state that a principal character is dying.

The novelist may handle characterization in various ways; an important distinction is between serious and comic treatment. Jane Austen's Mr Collins is a wonderful comic study of a pompous, smug, insensitive snob. We enjoy his absurdity; we recognize, caricatured in him—and with not all that much exaggeration—asininities we have seen in real life; we see, as plainly as in tragic treatment, the nature of selfishness: its self-deceptions, blindness and callousness. But he is conceived as a comic figure; we are not interested in his development as we are in that of Elizabeth, who is taken seriously. Jane Austen leaves us in no doubt that we are meant to find Charlotte Lucas's marriage to Mr Collins repugnant; but we are not invited to consider in detail what harm this nasty ass did to people near him; wife, children, parishioners, or how he must have failed those who sought his guidance. Pompous, self-righteous, unchristian clergymen are also portrayed in Mr Brocklehurst in *Jane Eyre*, Mr Casaubon in *Middlemarch*—but in the brief appearance of Mr Brocklehurst we see the real evil in such a man, his unfitness for power; in the much more subtle and lengthy treatment of Mr Casaubon we see not only his depressing effect on all around him, but his own tragedy: he is capable of pain and disappointment, he has at times reached feebly for something greater than himself. We feel some interest in how he came to be what he is, some sympathy that we do not feel when we just relish Mr Collins.

Almost any character or situation is open to either serious or comic treatment: there is a comic possibility even in alcoholism, insanity or war; conversely, there is enough real pain in mere social embarrassment to allow of serious treatment, as in *Evelina* or the novels of Jane Austen.

We soon see that not all characters in novels are even simple sketches of possible human beings: those in *The Pilgrim's Progress* are allegorical; Lemuel Gulliver is important not as a person, but as an observer of four imaginary countries that satirize human follies; 'K' in Kafka's *The Trial* is more an Everyman figure than an individual; J. R. R. Tolkien's *The Lord of the Rings*, though full of meaningful myths and implied moral truths, is not to be taken as a sample of everyday life or its characters as human; T. F. Powys's *Mr Weston's Good Wine*, though nearer to real life, is not a straightforward story of it. We realize that the characters are nothing like those in *Clarissa, Mansfield Park, Martin Chuzzlewit, The Return of the Native, Aaron's Rod*, or even, say, Agatha Christie's *Murder at the Vicarage*.

What is much harder to judge—and even experienced critics may argue about this—is how far characters are to be taken as pictures of individuals and how far they may have other functions. There are parallels in real life even to this: we do make private myths of other people; we are all apt to see persons as representatives, judging Pakistanis by one bus conductor, teachers by one traumatic experience at school, students by one mop of hair, beard and string of beads—misleadingly and harmfully. We meet someone briefly and notice only his mannerisms; consult someone and know him only in that fleeting relationship; fall in love and experience either a heightening of our perception and understanding of one person, or a dangerous blinding of our sane judgment—quite possibly both at once in relation to different aspects of the experience! The novelist, though of superior intelligence, is himself subject to all our usual psychological processes, and can portray life no more accurately than he can observe it. Even D. H. Lawrence, a master in many ways, was limited in his insights by generalizing from his own turbulent emotional life: he is a wonderful novelist of love-hate tensions, of struggles for dominance, of inner conflicts, of deep unreasoning passions; but he tells us little about the victories of rational co-operation, conscious compromise, healing humour, the courtesies of other kinds of love.

The novelist is not always aiming at simply a 'lifelike' picture. A photographer may put some objects in focus, sharply realistic, but have some objects in softer focus in the background; or he may choose to photograph something from an unusual angle, or to enlarge it enormously, so that a gas fire can become an inferno, some milk-bottle tops and a duster become demon eyes and monster fur, eternity be hinted in the tilt of an egg-cup. Similarly, the novelist not only selects and, as in life, gives his characters varying degrees of importance, but may use them as types, spokesmen, symbols, myths, hints, ornaments, secretaries, organizers, ears, criticisms or rhubarb-noises—and I am sure to have forgotten something.[1]

Great characters in novels are seen as complex human beings

and come to life as such, often with such vitality that it does not seem absurd to ask what they might do in other situations. (A scene between Lady Catherine de Bourgh and Mellors the gamekeeper would be fun; a more subtle exercise would be to confront Parson Adams of *Joseph Andrews* with the whisky-priest of *The Power and the Glory*.) The greatest created characters have a roundness, complexity and multiplicity; they develop, they give the impression that they had a real past, have a real future.

A lesser character may be a *type*: sensible housewife, brutal prison guard, unworldly scholar, man-about-town, gallant soldier, luscious temptress, poor old man; or perhaps a moral type—of quiet loving-kindness, unrestrained selfishness, weak indecisiveness, parental or marital tyranny, silliness, perseverance. He may be more a spokesman than a true character: express the viewpoint of a social class; articulate some moral or philosophical or religious concept; be a mouthpiece for the author's own views.

A character may have something of *symbol* or *myth*. If we read *A Christmas Carol* as we read *Silas Marner*, the characters will seem crude outlines and the story unreal; but if we read it as a myth or parable about the horrors of the shrivelled heart and the rehumanizing of the dehumanized, it is a fine one. *The Mill on the Floss* is largely a realistic story, but contains elements of myth: Maggie and Tom typify two styles of life and carry many overtones of universal problems. We can see them as Magdalen and Pharisee, Love and Law, Good and Right, Personality and Character, and so on. The characters in George Orwell's *1984* or Anthony Burgess's *A Clockwork Orange*—novels of ideas—are much more representative types than rounded characters. A gentler myth is Herbert Read's *The Green Child*.

The characters in much escapist fiction are types, or even low-level myths. We are all interested in the struggle of good and evil, and may wish it were as morally clear-cut as in detection against crime. The escapist novel cheers us partly by presenting clear-cut issues and typed characters about whom we know what to think; the great novel disturbs us by presenting either realistic characters typical of our complex humanity, or myths that are not crude simplifications, but images of the great, dim, echoing maze in which we move.

Characters may appear briefly as mere *hints*, bits of evidence: minor figures in *Alton Locke*, Reade's *It is Never Too Late to Mend*, Marcus Clarke's *For the Term of his Natural Life*, or *Uncle Tom's Cabin*, are there to show us what is going on. While this is especially likely in such reformist novels, persons for giving hints appear in many other novels: for instance, to give a background of vapid or witty, amiable or spiteful, conversation.

Minor characters, appearing once only, may be *ornaments*: the jocular waiter who eats most of David Copperfield's dinner, the innkeeper with his grievances in *The Cloister and the Hearth*, or Counsellor Kitch in *Lorna Doone*, who comes off second best when he tries to extract a fee from John Ridd. They are bonuses thrown in for our enjoyment.

Characters may be *secretaries* whose function is little more than to communicate something, such as Marlowe in Conrad's *Lord Jim*; or they can be *organizers*, not of much interest themselves, but causing things to happen; figures of authority in historical novels often function thus: the Duke of Wellington in *Charles O'Malley*, Sir Richard Grenville and Francis Drake in *Westward Ho!* A priest, doctor, policeman or lawyer often appears for such a purpose.

Some characters may be there chiefly as *ears*: an extreme example is Gilbert Markham's friend Halford in *The Tenant of Wildfell Hall*, who exists only as someone to whom letters are written. In *Wuthering Heights* Mr Lockwood's chief function is to be an ear.

Some characters are conceived mostly as *criticisms*: most of those in Wyndham Lewis's *Tarr* are exemplifying a style of life he detested, what he called the 'bourgeois-bohemian'. Mr Bumble in *Oliver Twist* and Mr Squeers in *Nicholas Nickleby* are intensely alive in their way, but are also criticisms of a society that could put such creatures into such positions.

Many novels contain very minor characters who function as *rhubarb-noises*: members of a mob, army, school, social gathering, meeting, whose remarks or actions give an impression of numbers, of large scale: we find them in scenes of riot in *Barnaby Rudge* or *Felix Holt*, or the burning of the books in Rex Warner's *The Professor*; in elections, trial scenes, executions, natural disasters; in scenes of battle; at dances, weddings, festivals. Different voices and varied reactions give the sense of numbers.

The pattern of hero and heroine, villain and perhaps villainess, the division into goodies and baddies, is typical more of escapist fiction than of the greatest novels—real life is rarely so simple.

A good character is more credible if he has some natural frailties, as is a bad character if he has some glimmer of goodness, or wins some slight sympathy by a clue as to why he is bad. In the field of character, one of the hardest tasks is to create someone good who is neither incredible nor insipid. Little Nell worries most readers; Oliver Twist worries some; Esther Summerson in *Bleak House*, trying to do her duty in a situation she does not understand, is more convincing, but some readers find her insipid. George Eliot is more skilled than most in portraying credible goodness. In following the details of Dinah Morris's tact as she consoles the widowed Lisabeth Bede, we see her quiet conquest of self. Daniel Deronda is a fine man, honourable, conscientious, compassionate, generous; but there is a wonderful stroke of truth to nature when Gwendolen wishes to tell him about the death of her cruel husband, and Daniel, who has plenty of problems of his own, does not want to be involved:

She was bent on confession, and he dreaded hearing her confession. Against his better will, he shrank from the task that was laid on him; he wished, and yet rebuked the wish as cowardly, that she could bury her secrets in her own bosom. He was not a priest. He dreaded the weight of this woman's soul flung upon his own with imploring dependence.

He tells Gwendolen he wants to help her: 'And all the while he felt as if he were putting his name to a blank paper which might be filled up terribly.' He is in fact kind, patient and helpful; but it does not come easily to him.

It is even harder for a twentieth-century novelist to portray a good character, when vulgarizations of psycho-analysis and of some schools of modern philosophy have encouraged a knowing cynicism. Graham Greene's Scobie in *The Heart of the Matter* truly tries to be unselfish, and risks eternal punishment to spare pain to others: he is convincing because his goodness is placed in such a setting of mistakes. Iris Murdoch is another modern novelist who can portray goodness in such a way that with all our fashionable knowing-ness we can believe in it: Tallis, in *A Fairly Honourable Defeat*, is generous, sincere, patient, unselfish, yet made convincing by his ridiculous and ineffectual side—and the ingratitude of his horrible father.

The recent conscious cult of the 'anti-hero', contrasting with the good, self-disciplined, resourceful Victorian hero, is not as original as may be supposed. Jim Dixon in *Lucky Jim* is the best-known example: we are invited to follow and sympathize with Jim, who is weak, silly, unworthy in motive, conscienceless in his responsible profession, selfish and greedy as we can all be, yet very ready to loathe and despise all the other third-raters around him. He is convincing and enter-taining; but in a sense anti-heroes are as early as Peregrine

Pickle or Jonathan Wild, or Lever's Charles O'Malley or Harry Lorrequer.

Minor characters may sometimes be more memorable than supposedly major ones: Dickens has several heroines not as colourful as Jenny Wren, Sairey Gamp, Mrs Gummidge, Betsey Trotwood. In *Ivanhoe* the official heroine is Rowena, but Rebecca is more interesting.

One of the most important aspects of the major novel is the interaction of characters. Contrasts are important: Henchard and Farfrae in *The Mayor of Casterbridge*; Dorothea and Rosamond in *Middlemarch*; Indians, liberal Britons and arrogant Britons in *A Passage to India*; Rupert Birkin and Gerald Crich in *Women in Love*; Jeremy and his father in *Strike the Father Dead*. Such contrast makes both figures more real; but the characters also act on one another and develop as a result of these interactions; which is often most of what a mainstream novel is about.

Not everyone has the same idea as to what makes a character lifelike, but perhaps we may say that in lifelike characters we find some complexity, a credible consistency, and either some normality in relation to the society in which they move, or some explanation of the deviance.

Complexity is part of being fully human. The skilled novelist shows the frailties of the good, the redeeming features of the bad, the doubts, perplexities, conflicts of duties and interests, the variety of reactions to people and situations; and a true picture of human complexity generally requires also some suggestion of an inner life: thoughts, motives, emotions, memories, perhaps fantasy.

Consistency is a delicate matter, because none of us is fully consistent—we are creatures of moods, cycles and competing priorities—but all of us are partly consistent. We can accept, in a fictional character, unusual behaviour due to shock; snapping of control under pressure; falling in love; unexpected riches or poverty; bodily or mental illness. But Dinah Morris under exceptional stress might weep, feel sick, even snap; she would not get drunk or pour out a torrent of obscene language. Jim Dixon could not take refuge in contemplative prayer, nor Jeanie Deans make money by blackmail. Thackeray has been blamed for suggesting that Becky Sharp hastened her husband's death, because, though she was a schemer, we have had no hint that she was likely to murder.

Normality is hard to define. We do, however, expect a character to be convincing in relation to his social position, occupation, education, family situation and so on. The dust-man may have any level of intelligence or goodness; but if he is brilliant we at least need to know why he is making so little obvious use of his intellect. A lawyer will use words more cautiously than a political agitator. A teacher may have feelings deep or shallow, kindly or spiteful, but can hardly be inarticulate. If the young waitress can speak Amharic, we need to know why, though she might easily have picked up some French.

In *The Inheritors*, set in pre-history, William Golding achieves an admirable verisimilitude in his primitive characters who are barely articulate, who live in a world of perceptions and emotions, yet are not without intelligence, reason or kindness. George Eliot, Jane Austen, Trollope, Meredith, Lawrence, Angus Wilson, concerned with people in complex societies, have to place each character in an appropriate setting of differentiated upbringing and experience and give him or her appropriate speech, manners, habits, memories, assumptions, limitations and freedoms.

Hard Times is full of sharply defined, consistent, memorable characters; yet it is also almost allegorical. Mr Gradgrind may stand for Reason when it takes the irrational position of rejecting other aspects of life. The denial of affection leads to the loss of morality: Bitzer demonstrates this. Mrs Gradgrind is Unreason: lost in bewildered whining, she shows that what Mr Gradgrind has is useful—he can do some

Character

things very sensibly; we are not the better for denying Reason and Fact; but Sissy Jupe stands for the Love and perhaps Intuition that Gradgrind lacks. Tom is Selfishness mitigated by neither reason nor affection—a warning of what we are all in danger of becoming. Mr Harthouse is a Tempter; Mr Sleary represents Fun, and, though he is no great artist, the circus suggests Art and Creativity. Stephen Blackpool stands for unselfish principle, for Goodness, but 'muddle' is his favourite word; Rachael is a Goodness, less questioning but more effectual; Stephen's wife exemplifies the wickedness that exploits goodness. Mrs Bounderby is an image of Uncon-ditional Love who paradoxically becomes a figure of retribu-tion, reminding us that to reject affection may set destructive forces at work. Mr Bounderby is a 'Bully of Humility'; Mrs Sparsit is more complex, combining Snobbery, Sycophancy, Hypocrisy and Malice. The one important character we cannot see as a personification is Louisa Gradgrind, who is a sort of Everywoman, the genuinely complex human being caught among various forces.

This allegorical aspect gives the novel a sense of univers-ality; but we also read it as a story of human beings. It is worthwhile to study Louisa's character; to see how Mr Gradgrind has some good qualities—he is mistaken, tied to his inadequate theories, he suffers a painful education. Mr Bounderby, wholly selfish and self-satisfied, is morally ineducable. Mrs Sparsit is not self-deceived—she knows what she is doing, and she has malice going beyond mere selfishness. It is rewarding to study how her relationship with Bounderby evolves, till at the end they mimic each other's sins to inflict final wounds. The reader may usefully examine not only Sissy Jupe's intuitive wisdom, but how she develops an authority which enables her to dismiss Harthouse and help others; or the details that show Tom's selfishness—such as his habit in talk of dismissing all questions of other people's happiness or convenience.

There are several minor characters whose functions are related mostly to the evolution of the plot; even Mr Jupe appears mainly in order that he may disappear and test Sissy's love.

Silas Marner is full of moral ideas, but does not have the almost allegorical element found in *Hard Times*. The most fully studied characters are Silas and Godfrey, both of whom undergo moral and emotional education; the reader will find it rewarding to study these, and to see how George Eliot makes them plausible by the first presentations of the characters. It would have done Dunstan Cass no good to find a lost child. Much can be learned, too, from examining the characters of Nancy Lammeter and Dolly Winthrop, and observing how some of the less thoroughly portrayed characters nevertheless have all the vitality and reality they need for their function: Squire Cass is a good example. We tend to think of this novel as one with few characters; but the observant reader should be able to list, besides those characters with substantial parts to play, at least thirty minor characters who add to the sense of solidity, the reality of village life.

One character leaves some room for criticism: William Dane, the member of Silas's chapel who really stole the dead deacon's money. He is possible: public commitment to an exacting religion is no guarantee of good character; indeed, his excess of loud religious self-confidence is suspicious: but his wickedness in not only stealing the money, but taking Silas's sweetheart from him and actively contributing to his disgrace, seems to require some hint of motive. The answer is perhaps that the book is *Silas Marner*, not *William Dane*; and it may be argued that the novel is no less lifelike because, as so often in life, we wonder, 'How could he?' The artistic need was to expose Silas to gross and incomprehensible injustice.

The characters portrayed most fully in *The Europeans* are

indeed the two 'Europeans' who come from outside and disturb an established pattern of life, and Gertrude and Charlotte, whose lives are modified. Much less is made of the mildly disreputable Clifford, who in another kind of novel—say by one of the Brontës—might have been a central figure. The cast is small. There are none of the amusing or pathetic miniatures Dickens or George Eliot paint so well. It is characteristic of James that when he mentions the ancient negress Azarina, of whom many novelists would make a lively, exotic figure, he does the opposite: Azarina makes her brief appearance in order to be less interesting than Eugenia had hoped! The reader should find it a valuable though difficult exercise to list the characters and define their functions in the story; to observe the number of interesting possibilities James refuses to exploit; and to see how, setting aside possibilities of being another kind of novelist, he concentrates on what he does best: to study a few people intensively, concentrating on the interplay and unfolding of character.

Anna of the Five Towns is indeed about Anna—Bennett's sympathies are with her all the time and all other characters are seen in relation to her. Her own sensitive, loving nature, doomed to stunted flowering like a lilac beside a chemical works, is portrayed with loving detail. In a sense Ephraim is the villain; he is given no sympathetic trait, though he is no stagey villain; he is horribly credible. The other characters fall roughly into two groups: those who are injured by Ephraim and with whom Anna is more or less concerned; a group of pleasant people who represent, and reveal to Anna, a more comfortable, cultured and gracious style of life. The reader will find it very illuminating to study the functions of the various characters, notably Mynors and Willie Price. There are many clever details, such as Mr Sutton's interest in archaeology—it is 'no use', it will make no money, its sole function is the growth of knowledge and enrichment of life—or the fact that the only creature that seems happy in Ephraim's blighting shadow is the one-eared cat, free of human needs. A large number of minor figures, such as the revivalist preacher or the girl decorating saucers, provide background and give the main characters the solidity of perspective.

In *The Secret Agent* three characters are seen under a microscope with a strong light: Adolf Verloc, Winnie Verloc, and Stevie. Winnie's mother is a secondary character; the anarchists and policemen mostly provide a background against which the four in Verloc's house act out their tragedy of almost Sophoclean intensity. In an ironical rather than romantic way, Winnie is the heroine, Stevie the hero, Verloc the villain, but all ineffectively: Verloc is a secret agent largely from laziness, and an incompetent one; Stevie has world-embracing compassion but no mental equipment to do any good, and it is arguable that he was not worth the sacrifices normal people made for him; Winnie's mother dooms herself to misery to no purpose; even Winnie's life of self-sacrifice fails. Intelligence and reason play little part anywhere; everyone fumbles.

An unusual and significant feature of this novel is that the minor characters are often more articulate than the central figures: the anarchists talk interminably; Heat, Vladimir, Toodles, even the cab driver who argues with Stevie, can put their cases, expound, argue; they form a chattering background of selfish and sometimes perverse noisiness for the tragedy of the half-articulate, until the sinister visitor to the house almost seems more impressive because he says so little. There is much talk, hardly any communication; much talk, little kind or useful activity. The reader may find it interesting to compare C. P. Snow's *The Sleep of Reason*, a novel quite different in plot and tone, but also touching on the horrors that follow an abandonment of rationality.

Numerous other figures provide a background of ordinary, solid, everyday reality: policemen, guests at parties, railway and steamer staff, whist partners and so on. By concentrating his analysis on a few major figures, Conrad gives the novel its hot, dark intensity; by providing a large cast of background figures, he gives a painful sense of how we are all affected by the movements of politics and society.

The reader who studies them will be left in no doubt that in these five novels, as in any good mainstream novel, characters are created and made to live; we must turn next to the question of how novelists impart life to their characters.

6

HOW CHARACTER IS REVEALED

The Hermit crossed his brow.
'Say quick,' he said, 'I bid thee say—
What manner of man art thou?'

S. T. Coleridge: *The Rime of the Ancient Mariner*

In real life, we are certain that John Doe is brave, if we have witnessed his courage, perhaps when he stopped two hooligans from bullying an old man. We may believe he is brave, because he has told us of his brave actions, or Richard Roe has told us, or he has a decoration for valour, or simply his manner and looks give an impression of courage.

We have to keep making rough-and-ready judgments of character on good or insufficient evidence. We may find it works pretty well if we take Bernard's judgment as sound, Alan's as sound except when it concerns clergymen, Tom's as well-meant but without much insight, Reginald's as unreliable, since he will say anything for effect. We know too that Bernard will hardly have a balanced view of Ronald, who ran away with Bernard's wife, and that while Tom's judgment is poor, his account of some event is probably honest. We also soon learn some humility: no final judgment on character is possible; we have to live on provisional assessments, but must keep doors ajar in our minds. We may modify an opinion when we learn that that short-tempered woman is in unremitting pain from arthritis, or that engagingly polite new neighbour is a good borrower but a bad returner.

Character in a novel is not as puzzling as character in real life: a novel is short; it is a work of art, so it is selective; the novelist must start with his own assumptions, preoccupations and experience. Yet we do learn about character in a novel rather as we do in real life: from people's actions, from what they say about themselves, from what others say about them. We may be told just what to think, or be left with some of the ambiguities and perplexities we feel in real life.

Suppose a novelist wishes to tell us that Leonard is kind and helpful, but physically awkward. Here are some of the ways in which he may communicate this simple notion.

1 *Direct statement*

'Leonard was always ready to help, but so clumsy that his help was often disastrous.'

2 *Direct statement in a fancier form*

'Leonard had a heart of gold, willing hands, ten thumbs and two left feet.'

3 *Direct statement in another fancy form—more literary*

'Leonard crashed and tangled his way through life like a sympathetic and biddable hurricane.'

4 *Direct statement by comic accumulation of detail*

'Leonard's heart was in the right place; but his head, arms, legs and bottom were frequently in the wrong place. He would rush to help a blind man at a busy corner, offer to carry old Mrs Varney's heavy basket; console Vanessa when he found her crying again; try to get any lost dog back to its owner or cat out of a tree; he never passed a car breakdown without asking if there was anything he could do; it was typical that, when Steve Croxton was ill and could eat nothing, then suddenly fancied quince jelly, it was Leonard who visited fifteen grocers and found a jar at the fifteenth. And never was there such a man for tripping over white sticks, dropping the contents of baskets, staining Vanessa's rugs with coffee, tying himself in leashes, bleeding from claws and twigs, oiling his suit, spannering his thumb, sparewheeling himself in the stomach. Even when Steve was better, no one dared to tell him how much that jar of jelly had cost: Leonard, craning towards a high shelf, slipped, fell over a trolley, tried to right himself, trollied himself to the deep-freeze, catapulted himself over and sat down in it, irreparably damaging fourteen pork pies, six scotch eggs and a swiss roll that was there by mistake.'

5 *Direct statement by the person himself*

' "I'm afraid I'm awfully clumsy," said Leonard. "I mean to help, but half the time I just barge about and make things worse".'

6 *Direct statement about the character by another person*

' "Leonard?" cried Steve. "Oh, one of the best; he'll do anything for anyone; took no end of trouble when I was ill. He'll help . . . but don't let him touch the Venetian glass; if he can break anything, he will".'

7 *Dramatization: the character shows his traits in action*

' "I'll be with you in ten minutes," said Leonard.

Vanessa heard the click and put down her own telephone. She blew her nose into a sixth tissue and tried to pull herself together, but was not much better when Leonard arrived, twenty minutes later.

"Hello–hello. Sorry I've been so slow—I ran smack into a bobby and he thought I'd done it on purpose, till he recognized me. I suppose it's your brother again?"

Vanessa nodded.

"He's a public menace. Let me get you some tea—you're trembling."

"No—don't bother—oh, well. . . ."

"You just sit quiet, and I'll bring you some in two shakes of a duck's tail." Leonard vanished into the kitchen, from which came, in succession, some practical-sounding clatter, a soft thumping which announced that he had tipped the potatoes out of the rack, and a crash as a saucepan fell; then Leonard appeared in triumph with a tray, on which were a teapot, two cups, a milk jug, a little loose milk, and a sugar basin adorned with an end from the tea packet.'

8 *Stream of consciousness: we are given an attempted representation of what is going through the character's mind*

Thus Leonard, in his garden:

'Sow lettuce here easy for kitchen soil not fine enough yet hello worm chuck that stone out rake it a bit more there's old Mrs Curnow signalling—oh, her tea-towel's blown off the line okay okay here it comes off the hydrangea—"Here it is, Mrs Curnow! Don't mention it! Nice morning!"—poor old sausage, she's getting frailer when I've sowed the lettuce I'll take her some of those logs now where did I put those seeds green and white packet ah it's blown towards the mint bed OW! blast! now what have I done stepped on the rake silly fool. . . .'

The fact that Leonard is kind but clumsy may also be conveyed in a way that serves a further purpose:

9 *Direct statement with oblique further revelation*

' "What, Len Hodge?" barked Major Crowe. "Hodge? No use for the fellow! Can't carry a basket up a hill without dropping something! Silly clown!"

"Oh, but he's got his good side," protested Mrs Crowe.

"He mowed Mr Hamilton's lawn every fortnight for ten weeks when Mr Hamilton was in hospital."

"And crashed the mower into an azalea! Tcha! Clumsy oaf! No use for him!" '

This also reveals that Major Crowe is harsh, intolerant and narrow, that his wife is milder and kinder, and that the marriage is not very happy. Character is often revealed by reactions to other characters; in real life most of us have at some time heard one person's comments on another as an illuminating *self*-revelation.

As in real life, not everything one character says of another will be true. The things said may be a *lie* or a sincere *mistake*; a *distortion* caused by emotion; an *exaggeration* for effect; a *projection* of some kind; a misleading *simplification*; a mere *sneer* from an envious or spiteful person, a mere *compliment* from a kindlier person; and so on. Misleadings as to character may be tragic or comic in effect. *Pride and Prejudice* is in part a story of comic misunderstandings of character (though Wickham's lies do some real mischief); in Hardy's *Far from the Madding Crowd* or Scott's *Kenilworth* mistakes and mis-representations have more tragic results.

The interplay of emotions affects what people say about each other: there are questions of tact, irritation, defensiveness, sexual or career rivalry, reticences, loyalties, inarticulateness, intimidation, propitiation, conflict between the generations, religious, political, racial or national prejudices. There must be scores of possible factors that modify our views of other people.

Then characters in novels, as in real life, frequently make mistakes in assessing themselves, through self-deception, inexperience, regrettably low or impossibly high standards, neurotic difficulties, pressures from other people, and so on. Gwendolen Harleth, Dorothea Casaubon, Felix Holt make painful voyages of self-discovery.

How character is revealed

A special aspect of character is often important in fiction. We know that life is so complex that in a group of reasonably truthful and sensible people there will still be ample scope for mistakes about character; mix in a few silly or malicious lies, some envious running-down and a few prejudices, and we have more mistakes. But, while all of us sometimes wear psychological masks for the sake of decency, manners, self-preservation, protecting others, and so on, some people deliberately set out to give false ideas of their characters—real deceivers or hypocrites. Strictly, the *hypocrite* is pretending to be virtuous when he is not, so we need another word, such as *deceiver* or *dissimulator*, for a person who is making some substantial pretence—of being rich, married, a countess, a graduate—but not feigning virtues.

Deceit, the effects of deceit, and the unmasking of deceit are such obviously interesting themes and so convenient for devising plots with surprises, that deceivers play a large part in fiction. When writing of a deceiver, the novelist may at first seek not to reveal character, but to conceal it, temporarily deceiving the reader too. This is normal in the minor craft of the detective story, but extends into the greatest fiction; or else the novelist may let the reader see the deceit from the beginning, and show the process and effects of deceiving.

The deceiver is not always wicked. A serious courtship almost always includes some element of deceiving and unmasking. The cynical aspect is common enough in fiction: in courtship we often cherish too rosy a picture of the beloved and of marriage. We tend to behave more pleasantly and generously than our average practice; and we may often be willing under the pressure of desire to give more to win someone than we can continue to give to keep that person. This need not involve wilful deceit. Being in love often includes elements of exaltation and heightened sensitivity that do enable us to behave better; the sad thing is that, unless a great deal of friendship is added to the excitement of sexual

93

love, the eventual quietening of the sexual urgency will bring our standards of considerateness down once more. Even Bounderby could for a time be somewhat softened by a request from Louisa. H. G. Wells treated this failure wryly but sympathetically several times, for example in *Love and Mr Lewisham*.

The less depressing aspect of this unconscious deceit is that all courtship, and indeed most friendship, is a process of mutual discovery. Serious novels treating of courtship or friendship often show this unfolding, stage by stage, of the knowledge of character and emotion. In very different ways Jane Austen and D. H. Lawrence present this brilliantly.

An obvious example of the deceiver who is a true hypocrite is Uriah Heep in *David Copperfield*. Though unattractive, he at first seems harmless, perhaps just neurotic; his full viciousness is exposed only in the fifty-seventh chapter. Less well-known is Ernest Gorse in Patrick Hamilton's *The West Pier*: we know from the start that he is evil, and almost want to shout a warning as he pretends to be affectionate and sensible in order to separate two ignorant but harmless young people who might have been happy together, and to trick the girl out of her savings. The deceiver's career is followed in the sequels, *Mr Stimpson and Mr Gorse* and *Unknown Assailant*.[1] The study is not very profound, but the detailed examination of how the wicked can exploit the merely silly is admirable. Another modern hypocrite worth study is Sinclair Lewis's nasty piece of work, Elmer Gantry.

A more subtle, even compassionate, study of a hypocrite is Mr Bulstrode in *Middlemarch*. He is puritanically high-minded to the point of being somewhat inhuman; his work is really useful and his life really austere, but he is too judgmental and moralistic. It is not until the fifty-third chapter that we learn, through the worthless blackmailer Raffles, that Bulstrode is rich partly by a wrong action; then, desperately trying to save his respectability, he deliberately lets his tormentor die by an error in medical treatment. Raffles deserves no sympathy. Bulstrode, cheat and near-murderer, is worth more; he has done some good and he cares for his family, but he proves to be a greater sinner than the ordinary frail human beings he so readily condemned.

George Eliot analyses, with subtlety, irony and depth, Bulstrode's inner conflicts, his self-deceptions, his bargainings with God, until we are left realizing that, though an ordinarily decent person cannot find much of Uriah Heep in himself, few of us can lay hand to heart and swear we have no trace of anything in common with Mr Bulstrode.

A benign deceiver is Mr Boffin in *Our Mutual Friend*. Dickens sees to it that for a time the reader, as well as the other characters, must believe that Mr Boffin is a cruel, heartless miser; later all learn how he has concealed his true character and invented a plot, based on his feigned wickedness, to save the innocent and expose villainy. Another benign deceiver is Paul Emmanuel in *Villette*. At first he seems dictatorial, capricious, irritable, rude; at his worst when he is contemptuous of Lucy's distress in attending on a cretin. Gradually we learn there is more to him: evidences of love, piety, magnanimity and generosity; he emerges in the end as a fine man, whose nervous irritability and intolerance in small matters are not surprising when he is under so much strain.

Actual *disguise*, or *mistaken identity*, are common in shallow tales of crime or espionage, but found also in major novels: Daniel Deronda finds out his real parentage and goes through a crisis of identity; in *Ivanhoe* both Richard the Lionheart and the young hero are disguised for a time; in *Little Dorrit* Mrs Clennam is found at last not to be Arthur Clennam's mother; the parentage of Oliver Twist is revealed only near the end of the story. Impersonations are important in *The Vicar of Wakefield* and *Pendennis*; questions of identity are essential to *The Woman in White*. A great novel turning largely upon such a question is *The Scarlet Letter*, with its slow discovery that the sensitive minister, Dimmesdale, is the father of Hester's child. Hester's lawful husband is also disguised.

The rise of psychoanalysis has led us to a more intelligent interest in why people are as they are: modern novels often search the past not so much for missing heirs as for missing motives. This has given rise to a new style in character revelation.

10 The quasi-psychoanalytical[2]

'Leonard Hodge's memories of his mother seemed to be full of a large brown leather carrier bag with carved bone handles. She was forever stuffing this bag with food, bandages, medicines, toys, as a preliminary to visiting neighbours in distress. Or she would send Leonard with scones to Mrs Tuttle, or ask him to help carry in Mrs Copestick's coal, or get him to amuse the Merriman children when Mr Merriman was in hospital again. The little games Mrs Hodge played with Leonard were all about helping someone: brave doctors and ambulance men and firemen, people with dogs on the Alps, people with camels saving dying travellers in the desert.

Mr Hodge had been plagued with over-sensitive nerves. He meant no unkindness, but the trenches in 1916 had left him a broken man. Shielding himself still from high explosives in the peaceful semi-detached suburban home, he would bark at a small boy, "Don't touch it!"—"You'll drop it!"—"Oh, do stop handling things!"—"Mind, you'll have it over!"'

Thus we see how Leonard came to be both helpful and awkward. Other authors may stress social or economic causes in our behaviour; others, biochemical factors, so far confined mostly to alcohol or drug addiction; others, genetic factors, as in Zola's novels of the Rougon-Macquart family.

How character is revealed

An example of the search for character formation in the past is Norman Mailer's *The Naked and the Dead*. This is a horrifying anti-war novel, in which we see men leading a miserable, dangerous, degrading life; we see sickening physical horrors, military authoritarianism, individual cynicism and purposelessness; but the novel soon proves to be more than an anti-war novel like, say, Remarque's *All Quiet on the Western Front*.

Most of Mailer's soldiers are revealed in their talk and behaviour as unlovable: ignorant, selfish, callous, narrow, brutally intolerant, lustful yet cold-hearted, sometimes obsessed by obviously silly interpretations of life such as that it is all the fault of the Jews. Then, in flashbacks, Mailer shows how these men have become such pigs, not only from the evils of war, but from past social and family handicaps: their destructive environments made emotional disasters, warped personalities and debasing patterns of life inevitable. Thus Mailer's novel becomes an indictment of some aspects of American civilization, though it is to the credit of America that he dared to write it. Novels influenced by depth psychology and modern sociology do not all have so wide a sweep: Scott Fitzgerald's *Tender is the Night* and Victoria Lucas's *The Bell Jar*[3] are among novels that treat of mental illness on a smaller scale, though at least the former implies a good deal of social criticism. Psychoanalytical influence has also encouraged the use of dreams, private symbols and fantasies to throw light on character. Dreams were used earlier—an interesting dream is found in *Alton Locke*—but later novelists go deeper into the irrationality and otherness of our unconscious. For example, Otto in Iris Murdoch's *The Italian Girl* often dreams he is trying to telephone but the telephone turns into something such as tissue paper or butterscotch; in *Pincher Martin* the distinction between dream or hallucination and objective realities is blurred; we find irruptions of extravagant fantasy in the novels of Kingsley

Amis or Agnar Mykle; or there are the morbid, magnified perceptions and waves of obsessive feeling in Sartre's *La Nausée*.

To treat in detail of the revelation of character in our five specimen novels would require a whole book as big as this, but some hints may help. In *Hard Times* Dickens deals mostly in strong outlines, bright colours, sometimes almost caricature, but with enough detail and subtlety to give solidity to the most important characters. The reader should consider the significance of Gradgrind's square finger, Bounderby's metallic laugh, Bitzer's blinking, Tom's pulling of rosebuds to pieces, and the images of suppressed fire in Louisa's thoughts. Dickens comments on people, but on the whole he reveals character by what people say and do. He relishes the disparities between what they profess and what they do. He can catch some feature of a character in very few words: there is, for instance, the masterly scene in which Mrs Sparsit gives Tom a meal only to extract information, and Tom accepts all he can get but does not trouble even to be civil. The fine dialogue between Gradgrind and Louisa when she seeks his help, and the equally fine one between Gradgrind and Bounderby, in which we see Gradgrind's integrity, care for Louisa, capacity to regret his mistakes, and genuine regard for that Reason he had merely overrated earlier, contrasted with Bounderby's total vulgarity and selfishness, are worth very close study. But the novel, in spite of a few irritating repetitions, is one of wonderful concentration, in which almost every sentence dealing with character, by comment, description, actions, or self-revealing conversation, contributes something to the total impression. (We must not forget that, though purposeless repetition is inartistic, making speakers repeat themselves may be part of character portrayal: it may show them as bores, or obsessed, of few ideas, fumbling, and so on.)

When George Eliot began to write novels, she lacked

confidence in her ability to write dialogue; this may be one reason why she wrote long passages of commentary. She introduces Silas in some six pages of description, which include the critical moments of the theft. At first it seems that she missed an opportunity for a more sensational scene, but all she wants is to show how Silas came to be wounded and isolated—for her theme is the healing of his psychic sickness. We can learn much of her technique by watching for her hints that Silas is only hurt, not really misanthropic; that Godfrey is more weak than wicked, whereas Dunstan is full of malice; that Nancy has both strengths and weaknesses. It is worthwhile to consider how the minor characters are differentiated, largely by what they say and how they say it, for in spite of her diffidence, George Eliot could often write splendid dialogue. And her direct descriptions are not cumbersome, but remarkably concentrated; for instance, the description of Molly and her past tells us something fresh in every sentence.

Henry James's treatment of character, even in his early novel *The Europeans*, is not quite like anything we have met in earlier novels; he builds up the impression of a character touch by touch, letting it unfold much as we gradually receive impressions of people in real life. He does sometimes make a comment:

> Felix was not a young man who troubled himself greatly about anything—least of all about the conditions of enjoyment. His faculty of enjoyment was so large, so unconsciously eager, that it may be said of it that it had a permanent advance upon embarrassment and sorrow. His sentient nature was intrinsically joyous, and novelty and change were in themselves a delight to him.

More often his characters keep some of the ambiguities of real life and are revealed by what they say and do, or what others may say, not always shrewdly, about them. We may notice how often when Henry James gives a direct third-person description of a character, we feel that the person is seen not by him, but by another character. The reader needs, moreover, to think about the characters as Felix does about his sister: 'There were several ways of understanding her: there was what she said, and there was what she meant; and there was something between the two, that was neither.'

Arnold Bennett's method of character portrayal is more like that of Dickens, with strong outlines and colours. He is also capable of unobtrusive hints, as when 'Willie Price stood somewhat apart', or, when Anna learned she was worth fifty thousand pounds, she went back to the kitchen and 'peeled the potatoes with more than her usual thrifty care'. There are fine touches of irony, as when Anna feels her sins as a huge burden—in her unselfish, hard life; and brilliant touches of detail, as when Anna tastes chocolates for the first time with Beatrice, who eats them as a matter of habit. An observant reader will find many examples of Bennett's skill in bringing out character in brief dialogues or quick touches of description.

In *The Secret Agent* Conrad tends to describe his major characters directly and at length, but, partly by his wry irony, gives the impression of being much more detached; even with Winnie he is not as sympathetically involved as Bennett is with Anna. He does also reveal character by what people say and do; and he makes great use of body language and physical details of speech: 'blinking at him steadily ...', 'the momentary drooping of his whole person ...', 'laid a long white forefinger on the edge of the desk ...', 'standing ponderously by the side of the armchair ...', 'the soldierly voice ...', 'pronounced mincingly ...', 'exaggerating the deliberation of his utterance to the utmost limits of possibility ...'. This emphasis on small indications of psychological states reinforces our sense of Conrad as a scientific observer. It is also illuminating to watch for Conrad's early hints before the climaxes come—Ossipon's practice of defrauding women, Winnie's fierceness as a child in defending her brother. The most masterly sequence of character revelation is the last interview between Verloc and his wife, in which Conrad shows how vast is the gulf between them.

7

CONVERSATION

The value of a sentence is in the personality which utters it, for
nothing new can be said by man or woman.

Joseph Conrad: *Nostromo*

Since novels are largely about human relationships, which
depend largely on communication, which takes place chiefly
through speech, conversation naturally plays a major part
in the mainstream novel. There are exceptions: Virginia
Woolf's *The Waves*, though using the word *said*, represents
thoughts, not talk; the people in *Rasselas* speak, but not in
the style of ordinary conversation. Conversely, the novels of
Ivy Compton-Burnett consist almost entirely of stylized
dialogue; but most mainstream novels alternate passages of
description, narrative or explanation with passages of
conversation.

The novelist is not restricted by the time-limit imposed on
the dramatist, but he faces one huge problem—he uses
conversation to throw light on character and carry a story
forward, and, at the same time, if he aims at verisimilitude,
he must make it seem like real-life talk. Yet a close imitation
of real talk would not do in a novel. Much of our daily talk
is almost meaningless: polite chat; matters of fleeting interest
such as deciding what to have for supper; repetitions, digressions, muddles. Our strong emotions are often expressed in
non-verbal sounds, about which we have few phonetic
conventions: is *Aaaah!* a scream of pain, a comfortable
noise after downing cool beer on a hot day, a yell of rage, or a
sound of tender affection?

Conversation

Most of us often have difficulty in expressing ourselves: we ramble, correct ourselves, try to talk of several things at once, suffer interruptions, try desperately to break awkward silences, talk about a triviality to avoid mentioning a real problem, and so on. Novelists do portray all kinds of flawed conversations: Jane Austen, a supreme mistress of elegant conciseness and precision, has also a wonderful talent for representing the talk of such people as the rambling bore Miss Bates, or the incurably illogical Mrs Bennett. A novelist may need to portray anything human; but a much higher percentage of fictional conversation than real-life conversation must have clear significance, and it must be rather more concentrated.

People in novels also tend to listen better than we do in real life. We do not pay full and continuous attention to all that is said to us; we develop polite tricks for seeming to listen to young children or tedious neighbours; we switch off attention because we are tired, worried, unwell; or we are thinking so hard about what we are going to say next, that we do not listen. The novelist may show all this; but in general characters in novels do listen and a conversation is a real exchange.

At the same time, a novelist must not select and tidy human talk so that the reader cannot possibly imagine it is real; and the continuous compromise, the delicate balancing act, between tedious realism and unnatural stylization must be very difficult. Here is an example of good fictional conversation; it is more concentrated than it would probably be in real life; but it is credible as human speech:

'Have you heard from her?' he asked as soon as Grey entered the dingy little room, not in Chancery Lane, but in its neighbourhood, which was allocated to him for his signing purposes.

'Yes,' said Grey, 'she has written to me.'

'And told you about her cousin George. I tried to hinder her from writing, but she is very wilful.'

'Why should you have hindered her? If the thing was to be told, it is better that it should be done at once.'

'But I hoped there might be an escape. I don't know what you think of all this, Grey, but it is the bitterest misfortune that I have known. And I've had some bitter things, too,' he added—thinking of that period of his life, when the work of which he was ashamed was first ordained as his future task.

'What is the escape that you hoped?' asked Grey.

'I hardly know. The whole thing seems to me to be so mad, that I partly trusted she would see the madness of it. I am not sure whether you know anything of my nephew George?' asked Mr Vavasor.

'Very little,' said Grey.

'I believe him to be utterly an adventurer,—a man without means and without principle,—upon the whole about as bad a man as you may meet. I give you my word, Grey, that I don't think I know a worse man. He's going to marry her for her money; then he will beggar her, after that he'll ill-treat her, and yet what can I do?'

'Prevent the marriage.'

'But how, my dear fellow? Prevent it! It's all very well to say that, and it's the very thing I want to do. But how am I to prevent it? She's as much her own master as you are yours. She can give him every shilling of her fortune tomorrow. How am I to prevent her from marrying him?'

'Let her give him every shilling of her fortune tomorrow,' said Grey.

'And what is she to do then?' asked Mr Vavasor.

'Then—then,—then,—then let her come to me,' said John Grey, and as he spoke there was the fragment of a tear in his eye, and the hint of a quiver in his voice. (Anthony Trollope: *Can You Forgive Her?*)

Conversation

Great intelligence does not always save a novelist from impossible conversation:

'Do you then declare against Parliamentary government?'

'Far from it: I look upon political change as the greatest of evils, for it comprehends all. But if we have no faith in the permanence of the existing settlement: if the very individuals who established it are, year after year, proposing their modifications or their reconstructions; so also, while we uphold what exists, ought we to prepare ourselves for the change we deem impending.

'Now I would not that either ourselves, or our fellow-citizens, should be taken unawares as in 1832, when the very men who opposed the Reform Bill offered contrary objections to it, which destroyed each other, so ignorant were they of its real character, its historical causes, its political consequences. We should now so act that, when the occasion arrives, we should clearly comprehend what we want, and have formed an opinion as to the best means by which that want must be supplied.

'For this purpose I would accustom the public mind to the contemplation of an existing though torpid power in the constitution, capable of removing our social grievances were we to transfer to it those prerogatives which the Parliament has gradually usurped, and used in a manner which had produced the present material and moral disorganization.' (Benjamin Disraeli: *Coningsby*)

And so on for pages and pages. Though, as Disraeli says at the beginning of the same chapter, 'There are few things in life more interesting than an unrestrained exchange of ideas with a congenial spirit', and though admittedly Coningsby is talking in Oriel College, Oxford, I doubt if even Disraeli himself talked like this! It sounds more like an Oxford student reading his essay to his tutor. It is fair to add that Disraeli often wrote much more natural conversation.

Conversation

When we try to judge an author's skills in presenting conversation in an old novel, we do not really know whether the conversation well represents that of the past epoch. Ordinary plain eighteenth-century prose is markedly different from ordinary plain twentieth-century prose; but we have no real records of ordinary talk;[1] this we can test only against other novels or dramas, and all must be to some extent compromises with reality. We cannot always even be sure about a conversation in a novel published this year, if the characters are speaking in an environment very different from our own.

The historical novelist has a special problem: to try to represent the speech of a bygone age so that it suggests the historical period, but is intelligible and credible. People cannot be made to speak Latin or Anglo-Saxon. Charles Reade in *The Cloister and the Hearth* achieved a wonderfully convincing mediaeval language, even differentiating for various nationalities; but it is a brilliantly tactful and learned invention, not a language that was ever spoken. Anya Seton in *Katherine* has made Chaucer and his contemporaries speak a language that shows her knowledge of that period; but if they spoke genuine Chaucerian English few readers would understand. It is doubtful if anyone worries over the obvious convention that, for instance, in an English novel set in mediaeval France the French characters speak English, modified to suggest the mediaeval. They must! But this kind of thing is a trifle disconcerting: ' "Donner and blitz!" was his first salutation, in a sort of German-French, which we can only imperfectly imitate, "why have you kept me dancing in attendance dis dree nights?" ' (Scott: *Quentin Durward*)

Science fiction frequently represents special diction—of another planet, of a hypothetical future, of non-humans; and Richard Adams very cleverly suggests a language for rabbits in *Watership Down*.

Traditionally, we accept some heightening, some lyrical

quality in speech, in scenes of great emotion; there are many such scenes in *Wuthering Heights*. This is partly a convention. like the operatic convention of the dying woman's aria requiring perfect breath control; words or song become symbols of inner experience, rather than naturalistic representations. It is not entirely convention: strong emotion often reduces us to broken phrases, but occasionally gives us more dignified speech. This speech itself may draw on our past reading; biblical reminiscences are very common at such moments.

We may welcome such heightened diction in a novel, because this is how we would like to be able to speak. In George Douglas's *The House with the Green Shutters*, a grim and economical tale of Scottish life, the conversation is mostly drably colloquial, but in crises it attains a kind of black lyricism:

'Janet! D'ye mind yon nicht langsyne when your faither came in wi' a terrible look in his een and struck me in the breist? Ay,' she whispered hoarsely, staring at the fire, 'he struck me in the breist. But I didna ken what it was for, Janet . . . No,' she shook her head, 'he never told me what it was for.'

'Ay, mother,' whispered Janet, 'I have mind o't.'

'Weel, an abscess o' some kind formed—I kenna weel what it was, but it gathered and broke, and gathered and broke, till my breist's near eaten awa' wi't. Look!' she cried, tearing open her bosom, and Janet's head flung back in horror and disgust.

'O mother!' she panted, 'was it that the wee clouts were for?'

'Ay, it was that,' said her mother. 'Mony a clout I had to wash, and mony a nicht I sat lonely be mysell, plaistering my withered breist. But I never let onybody ken,' she added with pride; 'Na-a-a, I never let onybody ken. When your faither nipped me wi' his tongue it nipped me wi' its pain, and, woman, it consoled me. "Ay, ay," I used to think, "gibe awa, gibe awa; but I hae a freend in my breist that'll end it some day." I likit to keep it to mysell. When it bit me it seemed to whisper I had a freend that nane o' them kenned o'—a freend that would deliver me! The mair he badgered me, the closer I hugged it; and when my he'rt was br'aking I enjoyed the pain o't.'

There is also a strong English tradition in both life and literature of irony, underplaying, reticence—both from fortitude and good taste, and from fear of warm-heartedness. Reticence can be moving, as we see in the best of Hemingway, in Jane Austen's self-controlled heroines, or here:

The service over, and the clergyman withdrawn, Mr Dombey looks round, demanding in a low voice, whether the person who has been requested to attend to receive instructions for the tablet, is there?

Someone comes forward, and says 'Yes.'

Mr Dombey intimates where he would have it placed; and shows him, with his hand upon the wall, the shape and size; and how it is to follow the memorial to the mother. Then, with his pencil, he writes out the inscription, and gives it to him adding, 'I wish to have it done at once.'

'It shall be done immediately, Sir.'

'There is really nothing to inscribe but name and age, you see.'

The man bows, glancing at the paper, but appears to hesitate. Mr Dombey, not observing his hesitation, turns away, and leads towards the porch.

'I beg your pardon, Sir'; a touch falls gently on his mourning cloak; 'but as you wish it done immediately, and it may be put in hand when I get back—'

'Well?'

'Will you be so good as to read it over again? I think there's a mistake.'

'Where?'

The statuary gives him back the paper, and points out, with his pocket rule, the words, 'beloved and only child'.

'It should be "son", I think, Sir?'

'You are right. Of course. Make the correction.'

The father, with a hastier step, pursues his way to the coach. When the other three, who follow closely, take their seats, his face is hidden for the first time—shaded by his cloak. (Charles Dickens: *Dombey and Son*)

With terrible economy, this shows the warping of Mr Dombey's mind; his daughter does not count.

Tape-recorder naturalism is neither possible nor desirable: but novelists have different ways of representing conversation, and conventions vary from period to period. For instance, it is amusing and enlightening to study a few sincere and serious love scenes from novels written at different times; a slangy style of speech today is probably a clue to easy, friendly, democratic sincerity; at one time it was more likely to imply conceit, immaturity and vulgarity. Anyone talking in a Victorian novel about the difficulties of family life with an honesty which would today be allowed a fully sympathetic character would then have been giving a clue to his insensitivity and depravity. At one time the speech put into the mouths of educated people showed signs of the customary classical education.

The novelist's own explanatory or narrative style may remain much the same throughout a book, except for changes of pace; but style in conversation has to vary almost from page to page, for the novelist must differentiate the characters —their talk must suit their sex, age, education, class, occupation, social life, nationality, religion, and so on. They may also have speech defects, mannerisms, favourite phrases;

some will be shy and inarticulate, some fluent and cogent, some merely loquacious; some witty, some dull; some may be prone to use vehement, emphatic language, or coarse and brutal language; some will be reticent or prim; some will like quotations, or slang, or proverbs; the talk of some will be muddled and inconsequential; some will have tact and some will not. Excellent examples of such differentiations will be found in the Bennett family in *Pride and Prejudice*.

People also talk in different situations: if some eminent scholars are discussing an intellectual controversy in a Camford common-room, and a cow walks in through the french window, the length, structure and vocabulary of the sentences used before and after this intrusion will markedly differ from one another. A man may be confident and eager when boasting of how he has tuned his engine, but at a loss for words when stopped for speeding. A man does not talk to his children as he does to the House of Commons. A formidable person's style of speech may be softened if he is in love. Speech habits change with maturity, education, success or failure, as well as such things as drunkenness, delirium, pain, old age, or prolonged isolation. Developments in character may involve significant changes in speech habits.

We enjoy fictional characters who have marked personal idiom: Miss Bates in *Emma*, or the conceited rattle of John Thorpe, in *Northanger Abbey*; the abbreviating, elliptical Mr Jingle in *The Pickwick Papers*; Mr Micawber with his misplaced rhetoric and polysyllables in *David Copperfield*. Here are a few less accessible examples.

A Londoner of low life:
'Vy now, I'll tell you, but don't be glimflashey. So you see, ven Judy died, and Harry was scragged, I vas the only von living who vas up to the secret; and vhen Mother Lob was a taking a drop to comfort her vhen Judy vent off, I hopens a great box in which poor Judy kept her duds

and rattleraps, and surely I finds at the bottom of the box hever so many letters and sich like—for I knew as ow they vas there; so I vhips there off and carries 'em ome with me, and soon arter Mother Lob sold me the box o' duds for two quids—'cause vy? I vas a rag merchant! So now, I solved, since the secret vas all in my hown keeping, to keep it tight as vinkey: for first, you sees as ow I vas afeard I should be hanged if I vent for to tell— cause vy?—I stole a vatch, and lots more, as vell as the hurchin; and next I vas afeard as ow the mother might come back and haunt me the same as Sall haunted Villy, for it was a orrid night ven her soul took ving.' (Bulwer Lytton: *Paul Clifford*)

When Andrew Fairservice, gardener at Osbaldistone Hall, talks with the Englishman, Frank Osbaldistone, Scott contrasts both Scots and southern, refined and uneducated speech:

'But you are no friend, I observe, to the ladies.'

'Na, by my troth, I keep up the first gardener's quarrel to them. They're fasheous bargains—aye crying for apricocks, pears, plums, and apples, summer and winter, without distinction o' seasons; but we hae nae slices o' the spare rib here, be praised for 't! except auld Martha, and she's weel eneugh pleased wi' the freedom o' the berry-bushes to her sister's weans, when they come to drink tea in a holiday in the housekeeper's room, and wi' a wheen codlings now and then for her ain private supper.'

'You forget your young mistress.'

'What mistress do I forget?—whae's that?'

'Your young mistress, Miss Vernon.'

'What! the lassie Vernon!—She's nae mistress o' mine, mon. I wish she was her ain mistress; and I wish she mayna be some other body's mistress or it's lang—She's a wild slip that!'

'Indeed!' said I, more interested than I cared to own to

myself, or to show to the fellow—'why, Andrew, you know all the secrets of this family.'

'If I ken them, I can keep them,' said Andrew; 'they winna work in my wame like barm in a barrel, I'se warrant ye. Miss Die is—but it's neither beef nor brose o' mine.' (*Rob Roy*)

A foreign accent may be represented:

'Goot! I haf now my own word to put in,' said Herr Grosse. 'It shall be one little word—no more. With my best compliments to Mr Sebrights, I set up against what he only thinks, what I—Grosse—with these hands of mine have done. The cataracts of Miss there, is a cataracts that I have cut into before, a cataracts that I have cured before. Now look!' He suddenly wheeled round to Lucilla, tucked up his cuffs, laid a forefinger of each hand on either side of her forehead, and softly turned down her eyelids with his two big thumbs. 'I pledge you my work as surgeon-optic,' he resumed, 'my knife shall let the light in here. This lofable-nice girls shall be more lofable-nicer than ever. My pretty Feench must be first in her best good health. She must next gif me my own ways with her— and then one, two, three—ping! my pretty Feench shall see!' He lifted Lucilla's eyes again as he said the last word— glared fiercely at her through his spectacles—gave her the loudest kiss, on the forehead, that I ever heard given in my life—laughed till the room rang again—and returned to his post as sentinel on guard over the Mayonnaise. 'Now,' cried Herr Grosse cheerfully, 'the talkings is all done. Gott be thanked, the eatings may begin!' (Wilkie Collins: *Poor Miss Finch*)

Professional and cultural preoccupations also modify speech habits, as in this sailor:

'Lookee, brother, your dogs having boarded me without

provocation, what I did was in my own defence. So you had best be civil, and let us shoot ahead clear of you.' Whether the young squire misinterpreted my uncle's desire of peace, or was enraged at the fate of his hounds beyond his usual pitch of resolution, I know not; but, he snatched a flail from one of his followers, and came with a shew of assaulting the lieutenant, who, putting himself in a posture of defence, proceeded thus: 'Lookee, you lubberly son of a w——e, if you come athwart me, 'ware your ginger-bread-work. I'll be foul of your quarter, d—n me.'

Once in the house, he presents Roderick thus:

'Your servant, your servant.—What chear, father? What chear? I suppose you don't know me—may-hap you don't —My name is Tom Bowling—and this here boy, you look as if you did not know him neither.—'tis like you mayn't.—He's new rigg'd, i'faith; his cloth don't shake in the mind so much as it won't to do. 'Tis my nephew, d'ye see, Roderick Random—your own flesh and blood, old gentleman. Don't lag a-stern, you dog!' (pulling me forward). (Tobias Smollett: *Roderick Random*)

Or here are two Members of Parliament, one Irish, one drunk:

'Och, botheration take your too-ra-laddy! Come, fait— by Jasus! clap your hat on and button your coat, and off to the House—immediately—or it's all up with us, an' out we go every mother's son of us—an' the bastely Tories 'll be in. Come! come! off wid ye, I say! I've a coach at the door—'
    'I—(hiccup) I shan't—can't—'pon my life.'
    'Och, off wid ye!— isn't it mad that Mr O'Gibbet is wid ye?'

'He's one eye—ah, ha!—and one leg—Too-ra-laddy,'
hiccupped the young senator.

'Divil burn me if I don't tie ye hand an' foot together!'
cried O'Doodle impetuously. 'What the divil have ye
been about wid that black eye o' yours, and—but I'll spake
about it in the coach. Off wid ye! Isn't time worth a
hundred pounds a minute—' (Samuel Warren: *Ten
Thousand a Year*)

Any reader should be able to collect numerous examples
of differentiations for emotions, moods and situations: a good
novel in which to start might be *Sense and Sensibility*.

Of course not all dialogue is direct communication; there
is not only lying or hypocrisy, but misunderstanding, which
may have many causes, such as the self-deception of inexperience, stupidity, emotions out of control, different
interpretations of the meaning of words, and so on. Here is a
conversation packed with gruesome ironies:

'Something has indeed befallen you, either in body or
mind, boy, for you are transformed, since the morning,
that I could not have known you for the same person. Have
you met with any accident?'

'No.'

'Have you seen anything out of the ordinary course of
nature?'

'No.'

'Then Satan, I fear, has been busy with you, tempting
you in no ordinary degree at this momentous crisis of
your life?'

My mind turned on my associate for the day, and the
idea that he might be an agent of the devil, had such an
effect on me, that I could make no answer.

'I see how it is,' said he; 'you are troubled in spirit,
and I have no doubt that the enemy of our salvation has

been busy with you. Tell me this, has he overcome you, or has he not?'

'He has not, my dear father,' said I. 'In the strength of the Lord, I hope I have withstood him. But indeed, if he has been busy with me, I knew it not. I have been conversant this day with one stranger only, whom I took rather for an angel of light.'

'It is one of the devil's most profound wiles to appear like one,' said my mother.

'Woman, hold thy peace!' said my reverend father; 'thou pretendest to teach what thou knowest not. Tell me this, boy: Did this stranger, with whom you met, adhere to the religious principles in which I have educated you?'

'Yes, to every one of them, in their fullest latitude,' said I.

'Then he was no agent of the wicked one with whom you held converse. . . .' (James Hogg: *Confessions of a Justified Sinner*)

But the mother is right! The narrator is to become a murderer through following his Calvinist theology to one possible logical conclusion. Most of us have seen examples of how religious belief can be warped into something more devilish than divine.

Trollope's *Barchester Towers* is full of amusing or pathetic ambiguities in dialogue, being largely a novel about misunderstandings. Here is true love in confusion:

He paused for a moment, and Eleanor's heart beat with painful violence within her as she waited for him to go on. 'I have esteemed you, do esteem you, as I never yet esteemed any woman. Think well of you? I never thought to think so well, so much of any human creature. Speak calumny of you! Insult you! Wilfully injure you! I wish it were my privilege to shield you from calumny, insult, and injury. Calumny! ah, me. 'Twere almost better that it were so. Better than to worship with a sinful worship;

sinful and vain also.' And then he walked along beside
her, with his hands clasped behind his back, looking down
on the grass beneath his feet, and utterly at a loss to express
his meaning. And Eleanor walked beside him determined
at least to give him no assistance. 'Ah me!' he uttered at
last, speaking rather to himself than to her. 'Ah me! these
Plumstead walks were pleasant enough, if one could have
but heart's ease; but without that the dull dead stones of
Oxford were far preferable; and St. Ewold's too; Mrs
Bold, I am beginning to think that I mistook myself when
I came hither. A Romish priest now would have escaped
all this. Oh, Father of heaven! how good for us would it
be, if thou couldest vouchsafe to us a certain rule.'

'And have we not a certain rule, Mr Arabin?'

'Yes—yes, surely: "Lead us not into temptation but
deliver us from evil." But what is temptation? what is
evil? Is this evil—is this temptation?'

Poor Mr Arabin! It would not come out of him, that
deep true love of his. He could not bring himself to utter
it in plain language that would require and demand an
answer. He knew not how to say to the woman by his
side, 'Since the fact is that you do not love that other man,
that you are not to be his wife, can you love me, will you
be my wife?' These were the words which were in his
heart, but with all his sighs he could not draw them to
his lips. He would have given anything, everything for
power to ask this simple question; but glib as was his
tongue in pulpits and on platforms, now he could not find
a word wherewith to express the plain wish of his heart.

And yet Eleanor understood this as thoroughly as though
he had declared his passion with all the elegant fluency of
a practised Lothario.

We find a different kind of irony in Angus Wilson's
The Middle Age of Mrs Eliot. Mrs Eliot has to work out a

new style of life when left poor and unprotected after her husband's death. In one of the most painful scenes in the book, Jill, another widow, heaps reproaches on her because Mrs Eliot tried—tactfully enough—to improve relations between Jill and her son-in-law. In a tirade of almost insane unfairness, Jill asks, 'Meg, what makes you think you can run other people's lives as though they were children? Are you so sure that everything you have done in your life has been so triumphantly for the best?' One irony is that it is Jill who is dogmatic, narrow, incurious about other view-points, embittered, sure she is right; Mrs Eliot is self-critical, trying not to become bitter, and trying for sincerity and self-knowledge. A greater irony is that through the novel Mrs Eliot has been the victim of kind, over-confident people who have tried to run her life as though she were a child. Advised, manipulated, scolded, she must have remembered with gratitude the principal of a secretarial college, who just gave her the facts she needed and said, 'Other people's suggestions are never much help.' Unfair judgment, and seeing our own glaring faults only in other people, are common ironies in both fiction and life.

Almost every mainstream novel includes examples of how strong emotion may modify speech, making it more eloquent, or less so, broken, confused, repetitive, exclamatory, poetic, even perhaps obscene or grotesque. Speech may also change to suggest serious illness:

'What will mother say? The bees are turning homeward for th' last time and we've a terrible long bit to go yet. See! here's a linnet's nest in this gorse-bush. The hen bird is on it. Look at her bright eyes, she won't stir. Ay! we mun hurry home. Won't mother be pleased with the bonny lot of heather we've got! Make haste, Sally, maybe we shall have cockles for supper. I saw th' cockle-man's donkey turn up our way fra' Arnside.'

... Alice's face changed: she looked sorrowful, almost penitent.

'O Sally! I wish we'd told her. She thinks we were in church all morning, and we've gone on deceiving her. If we'd told her at first how it was—how sweet th' hawthorn smelt through the open church door, and how we were on the last bench in the aisle, and how it were the first butterfly we'd seen this spring, and how it flew into the very church itself; oh! mother is so gentle, I wish we'd told her. I'll go to her next time she comes in sight, and say, "Mother, we were naughty last Sabbath".' (Elizabeth Gaskell: *Mary Barton*)

Rather a stylized and pretty delirium, representing thoughts rather than what a nurse might expect to hear so clearly; but touching in its context. Indeed, in Victorian novels there was quite a convention of deathbed scenes in which desperately ill people could talk remarkably cogently and audibly; but this is no further from reality than many other literary conventions.

One of the marks of a great novel is that we can turn to it again and again and still notice some masterstroke we had not noticed before. Close study will find in our five selected novels some interesting bit of subtle artistry on almost every page of dialogue.

Dickens achieves the intensity of *Hard Times* partly by making every speech characteristic of the speaker, not only in mannerisms—Bounderby's catch-phrases, Louisa's cool control until disaster breaks it, Stephen's muddle, Mrs Gradgrind's fatuity—but in content and emotion. Tom shows his callousness in minute details of speech as well as in action— no one ever matters to Tom but Tom; virtually everything Mrs Sparsit says is calculated; Gradgrind, as well as propounding his disastrously inadequate theories, shows some sense, decision and even kindness.

Conversation

Why does Mr Sleary lisp? Dickens likes the comic effects of faulty speech (we may compare Sam Weller, Mrs Gamp, Dora Copperfield); but possibly the lisp is a kind of phonetic equivalent of the clown's make-up. Sleary is uneducated, but stands for an important point of view; his imperfect speech may help to make his depth and articulateness in other respects more credible. Then the use of circus slang in the circus scenes gives a picture of a world alien to that of Gradgrind and Bounderby. It is characteristic that Bounderby merely sneers at the language of this alien world, whereas Gradgrind asks reasonable questions about it. Sissy Jupe's loving nature and fundamental wisdom come out in almost all she says—ironically, they are brought out when she thinks she is exposing her own stupidity! Mr Harthouse's smoothness of speech lets us see how, though he is shallow, he could attract Louisa, who must have had no courtesy from her husband and no endearments or fun in her home. And the great interviews of Louisa and her father are worth our closest study, weighing every word.

One of the merits of *Silas Marner* is the sympathetic skill with which a highly intellectual novelist represents rustic speech. She must have had a good ear for its sounds; she often makes it comic; but she does not deprive these unlettered people of either common sense or genuine emotions; she does not patronize them. She brings in many delightful touches of rustic, proverb-nourished imagery:

'You hardly know your own mind enough to make both your legs walk one way.'. . .

'I'm as ready as a mawkin can be—there's nothing awanting to frighten the crows, now I've got my ear-droppers in.'. . .

'The door was open, and it walked in over the snow, like as if it had been a little starved robin.'

Conversation

The conversation is generally alive, credible, varied, and
with few remarks that do not contribute to the revelation
of character or the progress of the story. Two points worth
mentioning are the skill with which Dunstan's criminal
viciousness is contrasted with Geoffrey's less brutal faults in
many little details of their talk; and the way in which people
whose only book-knowledge is the Bible often fall into
biblical turns of phrase: 'And he's took care of me and loved
me from the first, and I'll cleave to him as long as he lives,
and nobody shall ever come between him and me.'

The dialogue in *The Europeans* has not the obvious differentiation that we find in our other four authors. This is partly
because all the characters are refined, cultured people, polite,
articulate, and somewhat reserved. Yet there is some differentiation—compare, for instance, Felix and Mr Wentworth.
And the conversation is never just small-talk, though at first
reading some of it may seem to be; it is full of clues to
character, explanations (often implied rather than stated) and
moments critical in the emotional developments. It is, indeed,
about as concentrated as dialogue can be; this is one reason
why Henry James is difficult to read and an appreciation of
him comes later than an appreciation of, say, Charlotte
Brontë, Dickens or even Jane Austen. The reader may like
to study closely the crucial and complex dialogues in the
eighth chapter.

Why do Felix and Eugenia use so many French phrases
and Felix a little Italian? This shows them to be 'the
Europeans', and suggests much residence in Europe. Their
French is more elegant and convincing than that of many
French natives in English fiction: we realize they are at
least bilingual, and of cosmopolitan culture. The French
also strengthens that impression of the interestingly exotic
which appeals to Gertrude and worries Mr Wentworth.

Felix's artistic bent comes out in rather charming original
phrases, as when he says of Charlotte, 'She reminds me of a

pair of old-fashioned silver sugar-tongs', or describes Mr Wentworth's head as 'very mediaeval'.

All the time, in the subtle differences of phrasing, in the small cross-purposes, in the different values people take for granted, we are made to feel the tensions and surprises of this encounter of the Old World and the New.

Arnold Bennett's differentiation of character in conversation is a little like that of Dickens: his characters have very much their own linguistic mannerisms—Ephraim's ugly gracelessness, Agnes's youthful gush, Mynors's harmless polite pomposity, Beatrice's slight slanginess; Willie Price's first word is a stammered 'Ye-es'. We also find some of the characteristic diction of the Methodism of the period, and bits of Potteries dialect.

Bennett was noticeably fond of himself commenting on how people said things: ' "I haven't the least idea," Anna answered, with an effort after gaiety of tone . . .'. 'Then the minister said in a tone of oily politeness. . . .' He uses a great many words describing ways of speaking—'whispered', 'murmured', 'inquired', 'urged'—and his adverbs used to describe acts of speaking include: affectionately, angrily, blandly, briefly, calmly, carelessly, coldly, contemptuously, crossly, curtly, doubtfully, eagerly, earnestly, emphatically, enthusiastically, faintly, fiercely, foolishly, formally, gravely, grimly, gruffly, hopefully, imperturbably, jauntily, kindly, laconically, lamely, loudly, maternally, menacingly, mildly, naïvely, obsequiously, pleasantly, positively, proudly, quietly, savagely, scornfully, self-consciously, sharply, sincerely, sleepily, slowly, softly, solemnly, stiffly, timidly, warily, weakly, wearily, wildly, willingly! Bennett lays great emphasis on the significance of what people say, sometimes perhaps making too many comments.

The Potteries dialect is spoken by only four people: Ephraim, the elder Mr Price, Sarah Vodrey, and a workman on Mynors's pot-bank, though traces appear in the speech of Anna and others, and, though Bennett gives Willie Price only a touch of it, at the inquest it contrasts with 'the Kensingtonian accents of the coroner'. The younger generation, with more schooling, has more standardized speech. Bennett does not despise the dialect: only in Ephraim does the rough speech emphasize his brutality: ' "Humph!" the miser ejaculated. "That's better than a bat in the eye with a burnt stick." From him, this was the superlative of praise.' His inability ever to speak kindly to Anna is reinforced by his ugly diction; but his trouble is not want of standard English; it is want of love.

The conversations in *The Secret Agent* are worth studying as, half the time, examples of *non*-communication. People neither really talk nor really listen. This is most obvious as the anarchists ramble: they go on and on in hatred, contempt, destructiveness, but never have real discussion. (We could compare, say, some Fabians, or some modern non-violent anarchists planning a small commune; we might agree with them or not, but they would be communicating with one another and discussing constructive remedies and practical possibilities.)

Three conversations supremely worth studying are: that of Chief Inspector Heat and the Assistant Commissioner in Chapter 6, in which both are using their words at least as much to conceal as to reveal their thoughts; the ghastly last conversations of Verloc and his wife in Chapter 11, in which they are almost talking to themselves, and Verloc asks his staggeringly insensitive question 'Do be reasonable, Winnie. What would it have been if you had lost me?' and the final conversation between Mrs Verloc and Ossipon in Chapter 13, in which each seeks to manipulate the other for selfish ends, but Mrs Verloc is sincere in her terror and means to keep her bargain, whereas Ossipon is practising clever tricks of amorousness and reassurance while planning to take her money and forsake her.

Conversation

In this novel Conrad had to come to terms with the problem of foreigners' English. He made no attempt at phonetic representation of an accent. His own position was odd, in that his native tongue was Polish.[2] He frequently represents foreigners' English by giving them a certain pedantry or pomposity—an English correct but a little too good to be true. Privy Councillor Wurmt says, 'You are very corpulent', where most English people would use *fat* or *stout*, and probably say, 'How fat you are!' Vladimir, said to have 'guttural Asian tones', seeks for an idiomatic expression and comes out with, 'You shall be chucked'. Yundt knows the language well, but his enunciation is blurred. Ossipon uses rather more homely English idioms. Conrad also finds appropriate diction for police officers, a professional politician and others; he has to find an idiom for Stevie that is appropriate to a mental defective, but does not make him so sub-human as to lose our sympathy. This he achieves: we can feel concern over Stevie's just articulate thought and childlike goodwill, and see how in his feeble mind the ideas develop that make him vulnerable to Verloc's fatal manipulation.

Every speech in *The Secret Agent* is worth careful examination; there is much subtlety, powerful irony, economy. Here is just one ironical twist—Verloc, engaged in making a thorough mess of life, expresses specific contempt for a *language* skill: 'Who knows Latin? Only a few hundred imbeciles who aren't fit to take care of themselves.' This vulgar contempt for knowledge is also ironical: imbeciles are people like poor Stevie, who could never learn Latin, Verloc is eminently unfit to take care of himself; and in a small way it is symbolic: arrogant, dismissive, negative, Verloc welcomes the darkness of ignorance and intentionally rejects a form of communication.

In real life we sometimes hear people say someone 'talks like a book'. I have never heard an educated or sensitive person say this. Like many of our silliest remarks, it is prompted by

123

envy; it expresses contempt for someone who is more witty, articulate, thoughtful or informed. We certainly should not talk like escapist romances, whether in sentimental clichés or in a brutal manner that is inverted sentimentality, but by studying great novels we may learn much about both how not to talk to people, and how to talk usefully. It is always worthwhile to pick up some hints about the precise expression, courtesy, tact, conciseness, wit and grace in speech that save trouble or give pleasure to others.

8

SCENE AND BACKGROUND

> And as imagination bodies forth
> . The form of things unknown, the poet's pen
> Turns them to shapes, and gives to airy nothing
> A local habitation and a name.

Shakespeare: *A Midsummer Night's Dream*, Act V, Scene I

Human beings have experiences in very varied places: the high seas, the Yorkshire moors, the Canadian tundra, the tropical jungle, a mediaeval castle, modern factory, red-brick university, convent, prison, coal mine, power station, school, hospital, or even on the moon; but they cannot have them nowhere, so, though the novelist need not choose to provide a detailed background, he normally has to set his scene.

The background of a novel is also more than a backcloth for a drama; all novels, even the lightest, have some sociological implications; for, though the major novelist is most often interested in a fairly small number of human beings and their personal experiences and relationships, human beings do not exist independently of the society in which they live. A misfit or rebel is as much conditioned by the society in which he lives as is a dull conformist or mature compromiser. Even a tolerably free society puts heavy pressures on us, not because social organization is inherently evil, but because living together restricts everyone's clamorous selfishness, and yet we cannot avoid being interdependent. So novels are in part about our experiences in society, our problems of adjustment, how our environment modifies us, how we act on our environment. The background of a novel does not consist just of *scenery*, which indeed is rarely of paramount interest, but of the whole *environment*: the country, district, urban or rural location, climate, date, customs, economic level, occupational groups, buildings, diet, family patterns, religion, politics, moral assumptions, intellectual and cultural life, education, amusements, standard of living and so on.

The novelist has to build up this background with sufficient, but not tedious, detail. He may do some straight description, but most readers dislike too many unbroken passages of pure description. George Eliot, Dickens, Bennett and Lawrence are among those who describe backgrounds very well. The novelist can make characters talk about their environment. But he will also keep it in our minds by many small, consistent details. Do not, for instance, these alternative ways of quenching thirst already imply different environments?

1　'No,' said he, pouring himself a fresh goblet of mead. . . .
2　. . . as Daphnis poured him another cup of Samian wine. . . .
3　. . . sipping his grog. . . .
4　. . . reaching for the heavy cut-glass decanter. . . .
5　. . . buying a Coke from a vending machine. . . .
6　. . . swallowing another glass of mixed juices of organically grown vegetables. . . .
7　. . . gulping the flat recycled water. . . .
8　. . . nursing a mug of cocoa. . . .
9　. . . washing down the *sashimi* with a cup of warmed *sake*. . . .
10　. . . taking a third spoonful of beef-tea. . . .

Background may be on a large or small scale: we may have a picture of a city with its buildings, crowds, buses, but also a detailed picture of the inside of a house in the city—rich, comfortable or wretched, happy or full of irritations, elegant or tasteless or imaginative. The furniture of Poynton,

Scene and background

Waterbath and Ricks in Henry James's *The Spoils of Poynton* is highly significant. A novel may restrict its background to a small range of social levels (Jane Austen, Virginia Woolf) or cover a much wider panorama with contrasts of classes and backgrounds (Dickens, Tolstoy, Lawrence, Trollope).

The novelist may write of a background he knows very well, one he knows superficially or one he knows only by hearsay. All historical novels come in the third category. The serious historical novelist has to do something like scholarly research to get his background even approximately right, but every serious novelist has to do research in some sense; he often needs to read, enquire, verify details. Even when he knows the background well, he may now and then check a detail, if he thinks it matters. (Scholars have found Dickens sometimes wrong on details of Poor Law administration at a given date; he was never wrong about how callous and stupid officials can add to the misery of people in trouble.) In reading a novel, we may be excited by the story, sympathize with the characters, but take much of the background for granted; yet it probably cost the writer much effort.

Background is not of the same significance in all novels: there is less sociological observation or vivid naturalistic background in *Mrs Dalloway* or *Pamela* or *Jane Eyre* or Charles Williams's *Descent into Hell* than in *Middlemarch* or *The Return of the Native* or H. G. Wells's *Ann Veronica* or Trollope's *The Way We Live Now*; and different novelists use background differently.

It may just be *there*, as in light escapist novels of domestic life, and, to some extent, the great novels of Fielding, Richardson or Jane Austen; the background is well drawn, but what matters is the interplay of character and motive.

It may be more important than anything else, as in the novel of social protest, which portrays faults in society, character and plot being secondary to the reformist purpose, *Uncle Tom's Cabin*, Upton Sinclair's *The Jungle*, Ben Traven's

Scene and background

The Death Ship, Richard Dana's *Two Years Before the Mast*, Charles Kingsley's *Yeast* and *Alton Locke*, Marcus Clarke's *For the Term of his Natural Life*, Lewis Grassic Gibbon's *A Scots Quair*, John Steinbeck's *The Grapes of Wrath*, Mulk Raj Anand's *Coolie*, Alan Paton's *Cry, the Beloved Country*. A highly topical novel has a great immediate advantage, but seldom lasts longer than the evils it sought to expose, unless, like all those mentioned above, it has other merits. Negro slavery is gone and Mrs Stowe's religious assumptions are outdated; but *Uncle Tom's Cabin* remains worth reading, since it has some good dialogue, at least one really good character study—the selfish Marie St Clare, who, posing as sensitive and frail, is pathologically insensitive to everyone else's needs—and much that is still relevant to social problems, as when the high-principled and capable Miss Ophelia discovers the real problems of handling the delinquent Topsy. The best novels of protest have also a fairly broad and compassionate humanity and pay attention to the novel as a work of art; like Queen Victoria, few of us like to be addressed as if we were public meetings.

The temptation of the reformist novelist is to be too shrill, to forget the complexity of life: we should loathe cruelty and injustice, but not all employers, rich men, white men or even concentration camp guards are monsters; and there is no merit in turning a society upside down to create new patterns of oppressors and oppressed; the best society is the one with least oppression. (Black racism has now emerged and is as ugly as white racism; Jewish contempt for a *goy* (Gentile) is as ignoble as antisemitism, though both frailties are all too understandable in their historical perspective.)

Honesty compels me to add that some of the appeal of powerful protest novels, especially those no longer topical (such as *For the Term of his Natural Life*, with its horrible scenes of the flogging of convicts in Australia), may really be to sadistic feeling. It is hardly possible to expose cruelty, for the purpose of arousing reformist public opinion, without a risk of gratifying sadism, and even in the kind and sensitive, motives may be mixed. This, perhaps, we must just accept as inevitable, remembering that there are touches of sadism in many loving and harmless people, and that reading a book is one of the least objectionable ways of gratifying the interest.

A novelist may imply social criticisms by his portrayal of an environment, without writing an obvious protest novel—we may consider Trollope's novels of the political scene, or *Moll Flanders, Jonathan Wild, Bleak House, Agnes Grey*, J. B. Priestley's *Angel Pavement*, John Wain's *The Smaller Sky*, Mary McCarthy's *The Group*.

A background may also be portrayed as an *example*. This is the point of the invented background of all utopian novels, of which one of the most humane is Aldous Huxley's *Island*, which has a good deal of plot and characterization. Or it may be a *warning*, as in Jack London's *The Iron Heel*, Aldous Huxley's *Brave New World* or George Orwell's *1984*. Such novels extrapolate trends of an epoch to make their dangers clear. Then there are invented backgrounds that are more fantastic, such as those of H. G. Wells's *The First Men in the Moon*, David Lindsay's *A Voyage to Arcturus*, David Galouye's *Dark Universe* and hundreds of science-fiction or fantasy novels ranging from the brilliant to the worthless. Novels can have their own autonomous mythologies, such as Tolkien's *The Lord of the Rings*; or worlds that resemble the real world but are exaggerated for satirical purposes, as in *Candide* or Nathanael West's *A Cool Million*. T. H. White's strange and wonderful *The Once and Future King* mixes genuine historical learning with fantasy and even with modern psychological realism.

A slightly disguised realistic background is not invented in the same manner: Hardy's 'Wessex' is the Dorset and Wiltshire he knew, touched by his tragic imagination. Arnold Bennett's Five Towns are the Potteries, in which most

Scene and background

of the places and buildings he mentions can be identified; Mary Webb's 'Salop' is Shropshire; Trollope's Barsetshire is reminiscent of the area round Salisbury and Mrs Gaskell's Cranford was Knutsford, Cheshire; William Faulkner's Yoknapatawpha County is the North Mississippi area. Such disguises are a matter of prudence and tact.

In the background of a novel we may enjoy the pleasure of recognition or of the unfamiliar. One reason for Agatha Christie's appeal is that most of her novels are set in communities we find familiar; Ian Fleming succeeded partly by vividly sensuous portrayals of exotic backgrounds such as the Caribbean or Japan. He does not aim at truth: but his knowingness about details makes us think we are being told more than we are.[1] We can enjoy feeling, 'That's just what it's like!'—or, equally, 'Whew! How strange!'

All historical novels please in part by the unfamiliar background; but also a time comes when what was a novel of contemporary life loses the appeal of recognition and takes on the charm of the unfamiliar. Fielding, Jane Austen, Dickens, Trollope, are now mines of information for the student of history; but this was not their intention.

A writer can deliberately present an exotic background, as in Defoe's *Captain Singleton* (Africa) or *Colonel Jack* (Virginia); Aphra Behn's *Oroonoko* (Surinam); Mrs Radcliffe's *The Mysteries of Udolpho* (sixteenth-century France and Italy); Kingsley Amis's *I Like It Here* (Portugal); and Agnar Mykle's *Rubicon*, describing a young Norwegian's experience of Germany and France in the 1930s, vividly conveys the shock and thrill of a first trip abroad.

Since fiction is concerned with problems of human adjustment, a change of background may be an important part of the whole plot. The shift from Europe to America, or America to Europe, is a theme of great interest to Henry James; D. H. Lawrence's *The Plumed Serpent* and *Kangaroo* show the impact of alien civilizations in Mexico and Australia respectively. John Wain's *The Young Visitors* shows young Russians reacting to England. Disraeli in *Tancred* wrote of a quest for wisdom in Palestine; Dickens in *Martin Chuzzlewit* took his hero to America; Meredith in *Vittoria* wrote of the Italian nationalist movement of 1848. E. M. Forster's *A Passage to India* uses a framework of imperialism and the clash of cultures to treat of difficulties of understanding and the high price of integrity.

We cannot neatly divide serious novels into those inviting recognition and those providing the excitingly unfamiliar. When we read the novels of Tolstoy, Dostoievski, Gogol, Turgenev, we find the background exotic: samovars, steppe, cossacks, kvass, kasha, troikas and so on; but the Russian novelists were portraying the world they knew—presumably to a Russian reader of English novels bacon, cider, muffins and curates are exotic. Some Commonwealth writers who write in English and are admired in England may have double, or ambiguous, intentions: are they more interested in conveying a picture of the native land to the British reader, or in interpreting their environment to others who know it? We may think of V. S. Naipaul (Trinidad); Chinua Achebe (Nigeria), Sarah Gertrude Millin (South Africa), Patrick White (Australia), Mulk Raj Anand (India) and others.

All writers of any permanent significance will have readers who know the background and readers who do not. Some of my relish for Arnold Bennett is because I know the Potteries well, whereas the rural Shropshire of Mary Webb is a remoter world to me; but suppose I had my roots in rural Shropshire instead of having 'cum from wheer the mugs cum from' I should feel more recognition on reading Mary Webb and more unfamiliarity in the world of Bennett, though still respecting both.

What all experiences of a given novel have in common is an appreciation of instincts, needs and motives that are probably universal; of problems that, if not ours, have parallels in ours; of the importance of moral values and moral choices, though precise moral assumptions vary with time and place; we recognize truths of human experience not only in novelists as early as Richardson, but in Greek tragedy, the love poems of Catullus, the Indian fables of the *Panchatantra*, Chinese poems, African folk-tales. If humanity did not have a substantial common stock of experience, literature would be impossible.

In considering the background of a novel, we need to consider whether it is meant to portray the normal or the abnormal: is some description of poverty a specimen of 'the condition of England', or evidence that certain people have fallen into severe misfortune? Is a gigantic meal evidence of gluttony or ostentation, or what would be thought proper in a home of that class, locality and period? Is the young man with his mistress supposed to be depraved, or just behaving as his peers usually behave?

Locality is part of background: a country, a district, a town, a village; or something smaller: a farm, a house, a ship, a forest, even a sanatorium (Thomas Mann's *The Magic Mountain*), a leper colony (Graham Greene's *A Burnt-out Case*), a prison (Arthur Koestler's *Darkness at Noon*), or a mental hospital (Janet Frame's *Faces in the Water*). Then there is the social and economic background—one social group, or two or more in contrast. This is important in, for instance, Elizabeth Gaskell's *North and South*, George Moore's *Esther Waters*, and virtually all the novels of Dickens, and of some importance in most serious novels, since most of us have at least some wish for prosperity and some fear of poverty. The economic aspect of marriage may be as important as the emotional, the plot may even turn on the conflict between the two. This we find at least as late as John Braine's *Room at the Top* (1957).

Age-group may be a part of background: in most fiction

age-groups are mixed, but novels of childhood experience and student life exist. Many novels about children are written for children—about motives children can understand—but they include books of the calibre of Frances Hodgson Burnett's *The Secret Garden*, Rudyard Kipling's *Kim* and *The Jungle Book*, Eve Garnett's *The Family from One-End Street*, C. S. Lewis's Narnia stories, or Alan Garner's *The Owl Service*, which are better as literature than much fiction meant for adults. The world of childhood and adolescence is also a theme for adult novels such as Antonia White's *Frost in May*, the first two books of Compton Mackenzie's *Sinister Street*, Hugh Walpole's *Jeremy*, Denton Welch's *Maiden Voyage* and *In Youth is Pleasure*, L. P. Hartley's *The Shrimp and the Anemone*, Joyce Cary's *A House of Children*, and, in a different way, Henry James's *What Maisie Knew*, in which a child's viewpoint of adult life gives an unusual angle. The third book of *Sinister Street* is a picture of Oxford student life; Philip Larkin's *Jill* is a good later one; Elizabeth Bowen in *The Death of the Heart*, Emma Smith in *The Far Cry*, E. Arnot Robertson in *Ordinary Families*, Carson McCullers in *The Member of the Wedding* and J. D. Salinger in *The Catcher in the Rye* treat of the emotional perplexities of adolescence; *Tom Sawyer* and *Huckleberry Finn* are masterpieces of more primitive, less privileged youth; J. T. Farrell's *Young Lonigan* shows how an American youth, city Irish, with some potential for thought and feeling, is brutalized by narrow education, lies about sex, a fatuous family background and a rough urban environment; the 'beat' youth cult is portrayed in several novels, such as Jack Kerouac's *On the Road*. And we must not forget the horribly convincing children of *Lord of the Flies*, or one of the most famous of all novels of youth, Joyce's *Portrait of the Artist as a Young Man*.

Old age has had less attention, partly because all writers have memories of childhood, but first-hand knowledge of old age may come too late for artistic use. Besides, in the many pains of childhood and adolescence there is some hope; the great novel of reconciliation to ageing is yet to be written.[2] Muriel Spark's *Memento Mori* is set partly in an old people's hospital and treats of decrepitude and death. Conflict and misunderstanding between the generations is of course a very common fictional theme, but it is more than background.

Occupational background may be rich in detail; one of the major novels depending on a particular occupation is *Moby Dick*, the novel of whalers. The mass, possibly the excess, of detail gives the story a sense of authenticity and a convincing framework for the strange characters and Captain Ahab's pursuit. The realism also allows a few touches of humour to lighten a tragic story. Occupational backgrounds much favoured in fiction include medicine, which provides an interesting background for many good second-rate novels, such as A. J. Cronin's *The Citadel*, in a long tradition from works like Samuel Warren's episodic *Passages from the Diary of a Late Physician* and Charles Reade's much better *Hard Cash* and *A Woman-Hater* (which deal respectively with misuse of lunatic asylums and the struggles of a pioneer woman doctor); psychiatry and psychoanalysis, with their opportunities of character study, as in Nigel Balchin's *Mine own Executioner* or Phyllis Bottome's *Private Worlds*; nautical life, as in *Roderick Random*, Michael Scott's *Tom Cringle's Log*, the tales of Marryat, Melville's *White Jacket*, Edward Howard's *Rattlin the Reefer*, Nicholas Monsarrat's *The Cruel Sea* and Herman Wouk's *The Caine Mutiny*; the world of education, from C. P. Snow's dons to the infant teachers in Amis's *Take a Girl Like You*, from a preparatory school in Walpole's *Mr Perrin and Mr Traill* to a headmistress doing her job in the frame-work of local government procedures in Winifred Holtby's *South Riding*; the world of institutionalized religion, as in Trollope's *The Warden* (Church of England), Mrs Humphry Ward's *Robert Elsmere* (clergy with religious doubts), Graham Greene's *The Power and the Glory* (Catholics under persecu-

Scene and background

tion), Diderot's *La Religieuse* (convent, from extreme hostile viewpoint), Monica Baldwin's *The Called and the Chosen* (convent, from Catholic viewpoint), or Iris Murdoch's *The Bell* (phoney religious community set up beside a genuine one). But in Alex Comfort's *The Power House* we find a textile factory, a chemical works, a slaughterhouse and railway work; in Upton Sinclair's *King Coal*, miners; in Nathanael West's *The Day of the Locust*, the film industry; in John Wain's *Strike the Father Dead*, professional jazz; in George Moore's *A Mummer's Wife* and in J. B. Priestley's *The Good Companions*, travelling theatrical companies; in Charlotte Brontë's *Shirley*, the textile industry; in Charles Kingsley's *Yeast*, agricultural life. The best feature of many detective stories is the vivid portrayal of occupations, as in the light-hearted but valuable exposure of advertising in Dorothy Sayers's *Murder Must Advertise*.

Religion and race may be important: Catholic belief and practice in novels by Graham Greene and Evelyn Waugh, aspects of Methodism in Arnold Bennett, Anglican organization and controversy in Trollope, Judaism in the work of Israel Zangwill, Bernard Malamud, Isaac Bashevis Singer. Inter-racial questions are important in novels by Alan Paton, Nontando Jabavu and others. Black aspirations are coming to play an increasing part in literature, as in the novels of James Baldwin and Richard Wright. The cowboys-and-Indians theme is a favourite in very shallow escapist romance, but J. Fenimore Cooper and W. G. Simms treated the theme of the white man's collision with North American Indians more seriously, and some South American writers have treated parallel themes.

All novels inevitably make some ideological assumptions, and most serious novelists have a measure of broad ideological concern. Jane Austen tactfully suggests the value of discretion, dignity, rationality, self-control, good taste; George Eliot shows her concern for unselfishness, integrity, acceptance of responsibility; Dickens favours love, kindness, individuality, sanity, good humour, as against bureaucracy, callousness, greed, selfishness, neuroticism. More overt are Mrs Gaskell's purposeful insistence on social problems and on the need for tolerance and communication; Charles Kingsley's interpretations of Christianity as applied to social questions; Chesterton's Catholicism and his affirmation of wonder, praise and the poetry of life. A novel usually loses in artistic quality when it becomes too propagandist: Disraeli, who at his best, as in *Sybil*, could give a story life and charm, was apt to use his novels clumsily as vehicles for political ideas; Lawrence sadly overdid theorizings that were much less illuminating than his evocations of atmosphere, emotion and personality. Eventually the didactic novel sinks below the level of literature: E. W. Farrar's *Eric* is an example of a Christian novel written for the Edification of the Young, and there are Soviet novels just as one-sided and foolish. We all take sides; but great art, at least in a form as complex and large as the novel, can scarcely work in blinkers.[3]

The details of background add to the sense of reality, of three-dimensionality; but the background may also have a symbolic function. *Moby Dick* is not just a tale of whale-hunting, it is a kind of myth. Melville said his whale had been 'broiled in hell-fire', and critics have interpreted the myth in various ways: the whale may be Evil, or God, Truth, or Innocence; it is not a simple allegory, and people tend to read into it something of their own conflicts and sense of awe before life's mysteries. In Saul Bellow's *Henderson the Rain King*, Bellow's Africa is as much a territory of the mind as a geographical area; the hero moves towards insight, a spiritual explorer making a spiritual journey.

Malcolm Lowry's *Under the Volcano* is set in Mexico, with the macabre customs of the Day of the Dead (such as skull-shaped sweetmeats), various details of poverty, inefficiency and squalor, derelict buildings falling to pieces, a once happy home neglected with the garden run wild, all building up the background against which Geoffrey Firmin drinks his way to final disaster. He mentions his concept of Eden and the Fall; a fairground wheel is in Spanish an 'infernal machine'; Firmin dabbles in research into the occult; a street is called The Street of the Land of Fire; there are volcanoes. Mexico is vividly presented as a real country, but again it is also a country of the mind, a symbol of disintegration and self-destruction. In a letter Firmin says, 'the name of this land is hell. It is not Mexico of course but in the heart.'

The language difficulty gives local colour—Spanish speakers dislocate English amusingly; there is a hilariously funny restaurant menu; numerous Spanish phrases are used— but language misunderstandings come to represent a whole world of non-communication and incomprehension, until Firmin is shot with the weird, comic mistake, 'You are a spider' (i.e. spy). An alien background is the setting for an alienated man.

In Conrad's *Heart of Darkness* the impenetrable tropical forest suggests the powers of darkness—the mystery of the uncivilized and the world of irrationality. The Nigerian background in Joyce Cary's *Aissa Saved* serves a rather different purpose: mission Christianity encounters paganism and Islam. There are conflicts of values and assumptions, but the central theme is the interpretation by primitive minds of an unfamiliar religion in the light of their own religious concepts. The resultant misunderstandings lead to the literal sacrifice of a baby to Jesus, then to Aissa's martyrdom. The picture of misapprehensions, *naïveté* (not confined to Africans), cruelty and unreason has ironical overtones; few sophisticated European churchgoers take their Christianity as seriously as poor misguided Aissa. The African background is not just an exotic backcloth, but essential to the study of the different mentalities.

The use of the Australian background in D. H. Lawrence's

Kangaroo is more complex. It is a beautiful picture of the Australian scene: scenery, climate, flora, fauna, natural vastness and beauty. On this Man has imposed himself rather messily, with ramshackle dwellings and litter. Lawrence gives a vivid picture of differences between English and Australian manners; the new style of life forces Somers (who represents Lawrence) to rethink some of his ideas. The Australian background stands for both the friendly, easy, likeable side of democracy, and the slovenly, sloppy aspect which Lawrence hated—the inefficiency, mess, condoned stupidities, lack of culture and inability to respect people or achievements really deserving respect. At the end Somers remains ambivalent about Australia.

Coketown in *Hard Times* is an ugly industrial town: it has overtones of moral ugliness. Louisa uses the Coketown chimneys as a symbol of her own psychological state: 'There seems to be nothing there but languid and monotonous smoke. Yet when the night comes, Fire bursts out, father!' The derelict part of the industrial scene is even worse. Smaller scenes, too, may be both realistic and symbolic: the confused cheerfulness of the circus background; the wood, full of worms, snails and slugs, in which Mrs Sparsit spies on Louisa; Mr Bounderby's home, Mr Gradgrind's 'great square house', and so on.

In *Silas Marner* the village of Raveloe is portrayed with affection and telling detail. Little touches of rustic life and speech often give relief, and Lantern Yard is contrasted with Raveloe. The fog, rain and snow early in the story are needed for the plot; there is sunshine at the end; the symbolic fitness is obvious.

The background of *The Europeans* is seen largely through the eyes of the Europeans. We are not shown much detail of the Wentworth home, but many clues give an atmosphere of well-to-do comfort, refinement, dignity and subdued good taste. There is space, privacy, leisure. Emotions are at least not poisoned by money worries. Yet James also subtly suggests the curious want of joy, fun or happiness in this wealthy home, the puritanism that touches it to greyness, and in which Felix and Eugenia make a breach. The details of Acton's handsome house make the temptation to Eugenia understandable.

Bennett gives a very vivid picture of the Potteries, including an excellent description of a pot-bank. There is sometimes an almost poetic quality in the descriptions of an ugly, drab scene that is yet full of vitality. Bennett is also expert at convincing details of furniture, business, factories, practical arrangements of life, little indications of culture or comfort. The plentiful details of the trip to the Isle of Man show how for Anna it was a revelatory experience; a grimmer revelation comes in the details of the inquest on Titus Price.

The background of *The Secret Agent* is mostly one of shabby, furtive city life. The descriptions are vividly realistic, but often have odd, somewhat symbolic touches: a *guilty-looking* cat; a *cracked* bell in the Verloc home; 'the *sepulchral* silence of the great *blind* pile of bricks near a river . . .'; the speaking-tubes *resembling snakes*; '*blind* houses and *unfeeling* stones'. The background is more one of an atmosphere, as in Dickens, than of a locality, as seen by George Eliot or Arnold Bennett.

9

DOMINANT THEMES

That fayre Idea shee doth live by thee.

Michael Drayton

In each of our five novels we can find some main theme or themes.

In *Hard Times* Dickens almost insists on his main theme too much. It is Mr Gradgrind's discovery that 'there is a wisdom of the Head, and there is a wisdom of the Heart'. Dickens was combating a narrow form of utilitarianism: *Hard Times* reminds us that love, sympathy, generosity, as well as art, amusement and imagination, are vitally necessary complements to reason, intellect and self-interest. George Eliot herself states the dominant theme of *Silas Marner*:

> But yet men are led away from threatening destruction: a hand is put into theirs, which leads them forth gently towards a calm and bright land, so that they look no more backward; and the hand may be a little child's.

A secondary theme is the need for integrity, the avoidance of dangerous self-deception. It is not so easy to define a theme in *The Europeans*; the whole nature of James's technique makes sharp definitions difficult; but perhaps we may say that the novel treats of the impact of Europe with its older and more complex culture on rawer America and its puritan tradition, and the impact of the Americans on the Europeans. *Anna of the Five Towns* is a study of a woman's spiritual education, her struggle to do right in difficult circumstances and the inevitability that her life must be one of endless self-sacrifice without even credit for it. Her sufferings and moral victories provide the main theme. *The Secret Agent* is more perplexing. I find three themes in it—non-communication, discussed earlier; the grandeur of self-sacrificing love and its great cost; and the theme summed up bitterly as: 'The way of even the most justifiable revolutions is prepared by personal impulses disguised into creeds.'

It would be too rash a generalization to say that every serious novel has some dominant theme; but it is often both possible and helpful to find one. It is more difficult in the more complex novels: what is the main theme of *Middlemarch*? Perhaps we may say that it is a novel about the marriage partnership: the importance of realistic expectations and wise choice, and of true partnership. With the two principal couples we may include Bulstrode, the Vincys, Celia, and so on, if we call the novel a study of the need for integrity. *The Way we Live Now*, another complex novel, has running through it the concept of moral failure in pursuit of worldly success; or perhaps it is a study of falsity, coldness of heart, and unscrupulousness in morally inadequate people.

We have episodic novels: the tale of a quest (*Quentin Durward, Joseph Andrews*); the true picaresque novel dealing with the adventures of a rogue (*Moll Flanders, Jonathan Wild*, Lesage's *Gil Blas*) or the lengthy history of several persons with adventures and great turns of fortune (*Tom Jones, The Cloister and the Hearth*, Saul Bellow's *The Adventures of Augie March*); such histories are something like epic or saga. We can seldom define such a novel by some moral concept: *Peregrine Pickle* is about the adventures of Peregrine Pickle. A personality or group of personalities is perhaps the theme of such novels.

The reformist or philosophical novel usually has a dominant theme lending itself to sharper definition. George Gissing's *New Grub Street* and George Orwell's *Keep the Aspidistra*

Flying are fine studies of how poverty batters an artist and threatens his integrity, and how poverty does not just cause material inconveniences, but poisons our personal relationships, undermines our dignity, deprives us of cultural opportunities and tends to bring out the worst in us. Zola's *L'Assommoir* is largely a study of the effects of excessive drinking. Mrs Gaskell's *Ruth* is a plea, very brave in her day, for decent treatment of the unmarried mother; Wilkie Collins in *No Name* exposed the injustice of the law to illegitimate children, and attacked vivisection in *Heart and Science*; H. G. Wells's *Tono-Bungay* is in part about the patent medicine racket; Richard Stern's *Golk* treats some of the absurdities of the television world.

While every novel implies some sort of philosophy of life in the popular sense, there have been a few specifically philosophical novels: William Godwin's *Caleb Williams* is related to his principles as expounded in *Political Justice*; Jean-Paul Sartre's novels are related to his existentialism, and so on.

There may be more eccentric dominant themes: a novel may be a parody, such as Stella Gibbons's *Cold Comfort Farm* or Michael and Mollie Hardwick's *The Private Life of Sherlock Holmes*. Max Beerbohm's *Zuleika Dobson* has the theme of many romances, the woman who is overwhelmingly alluring to men; but it is a *reductio ad absurdum*, to which he adds an evocation of the Oxford he knew and a collection of literary and linguistic jokes. There may be a comic dominant theme— that of Jerome K. Jerome's *Three Men in a Boat* is perhaps the general cussedness of small things; most readers probably regret the sentimental interpolations. 'Cuthbert Bede' in *The Adventures of Mr Verdant Green* has as his theme the flair of a young undergraduate for putting his foot in it in a world with unfamiliar customs.

Good science fiction often has an idea as its dominant theme: a new invention, an unfamiliar phenomenon, the extrapolation of a trend. John Wyndham's *The Midwich Cuckoos* treats of telepathic beings who have a collective mental life; H. G. Wells's *The Food of the Gods* treats of a modification of the growth process; Mary Shelley's *Frankenstein* was an early treatment of the still popular theme of the humanoid man-made creature. But in these, and in most good novels of this type, the real interest is in the impact of the unfamiliar on human beings and their society. The reader can perhaps think of other kinds of theme.

How far is it worthwhile to define such a theme? Obviously it may be useful to people working for examinations; but—apart from the fact that even examinations have for a good many people given the first push into worlds of worthwhile knowledge—it may also be a help to our intelligent, and thus more enjoyable, reading.

Henry James's *The Ambassadors* is beautiful, subtle, profound; but it makes great demands on the reader, partly because so much is conveyed by indirect methods, partly because James, in his passionate striving for perfect exactitude, sometimes writes like this:

> It was on the cards that the child might be tremulously in love, and this conviction now flickered up not a bit the less for his disliking to think of it, for its being, in a complicated situation, a complication the more, and for something indescribable in Mamie, something, at all events, that his own mind straightway lent her, something that gave her value, gave her intensity and purpose as the symbol of an opposition.

—a sentence that does mean something, but makes most readers pant in pursuit of meaning. (Though James has sometimes an easier charm, as when he hits off a nice simple French supper as 'something fried and felicitous, washed down with authentic wine'.)

We grow intellectually by stretching, and, if we are mature

enough to cope with it at all, we may gain a great deal by reading *The Ambassadors*; but it helps if we identify a dominant theme and hold on to that. The story is about a rather endearing American, Strether, kind, courteous and intelligent but a bit starchy, who is sent by his wealthy intended second wife to France to rescue her son Chad, who is 'entangled' with a 'wicked woman'. However, in France Strether discovers aspects of civilized living that are new to him, then finds Chad's mistress to be sweet, charming, good for Chad and having her own sincere feelings; he eventually finds himself urging Chad not to forsake so lovable a woman. By his honesty in admitting that experience has made him change his mind, Strether loses a rich wife and suffers much embarrassment; but he has grown, at a time of life when it is easy to stop growing. It helps when we see that the dominant theme of this novel is one that for many of us is at some time a tragic discovery: that there are various kinds and levels of duty. Strether is much concerned to do right, and grows towards a deeper sense of the elusiveness of right. This is an absurdly simple interpretation of a complex novel; but it does help us to follow it; much as the coloured lights on the London Underground help us to keep to the right route, though only trains can take us to Euston or Victoria.

Can we define such a theme for every good novel? Probably not, and we should not strain after one too hard. We cannot find a themeless novel, for it is impossible to write sense that is not about something; but we may find a novel with so many themes that we take it chiefly as a panorama of life. *Pamela* has a dominant theme more obviously than *Tom Jones*; Tolstoy's *Resurrection* than his *War and Peace*; Conrad's *Typhoon* than his *Nostromo*. What we shall find in every novel is a *selection*, a picking out of some aspect of life for attention, and a *proportion*. Earning a living, and sleeping, which between them take about two-thirds of most people's time, may well be mentioned only fleetingly in a long, good and even realistic novel. Love, friendship, and other encounters with the more exciting aspects of life, will usually be given their subjective importance, not the mathematically quantifiable importance measured by the time spent on them. We may say that here the novelist is preserving a proportion true to our own real experience; some may like to say he is working in eternity rather than in clock-time.

What is most interesting in life will not of course be the same for all novelists: there are few overlaps between Hemingway and Henry James, Smollett and Virginia Woolf, even Arnold Bennett and C. P. Snow; but we can, in life or in literature, learn a good deal about life by discovering what other people find important in it.

Sometimes we may wonder if we are 'spoiling' a work of art by taking it to pieces. There are times when our best response to a work of art is an eager personal surrender to it. Yet we do sometimes achieve a more thrilling experience by study, analysis, enquiry, reflection. When we find the study of a 'set book' boring, we may be failing in real, reverent attention; the atmosphere may be unhappy; or we may be continuing to chew over a book from which we can now extract nothing more, though in ten years we may return to it with maturer perceptions. But real study, like real love, is largely a matter of very close and sympathetic attention; and in both the rewards of what at first seems difficult may prove to be unexpectedly magnificent.

OFF THE BEATEN TRACK

I'm sure you remember all the characteristics of the modern novel, since you worked them up for the first hour test. I know you won't get it confused with the Victorian novel, which is inter-class mobility, the wisdom of the heart, the Darwinian Revolution, Herbert Spencer, the twilight of religion, tears, idle tears, and the responsibility of Empire. What I'm talking about is the vanishing hero, alienation, Angst, symbolism, the interior mono-logue and the stream of consciousness.

'Professor Murphy A. Sweat' in
Frederick C. Crews: *The Pooh Perplex*[1]

I have kept using the loose term 'mainstream novel', to avoid a clutter of exceptions and reservations; it cannot be defined as sharply as *beryllium* or *hexagon*, but we have some general notion of it as a novel in which fairly realistic human characters, in credible environments, react to and act on one another, with recognizable human motives, in a time sequence we can easily grasp. Most of us would class as mainstream novelists Fielding, Scott, Jane Austen, the Brontës, Dickens, Trollope, Conrad, Elizabeth Bowen, Angus Wilson and even Saul Bellow; and regard Virginia Woolf, James Joyce and William Burroughs as in another class. Or we may prefer to speak of the 'traditional' and the 'experimental' novel.

Probably most of us, at some stage in our reading adven-tures, develop some vague concept of the mainstream novel as a good solid tale of characters and events, with enough suspense to keep us going and enough thoughtful examination of life to be more than just a harmless way of killing time: a readable tale with a beginning, a middle and an end—a tasty, nourishing and satisfying meaty mental meal. Then one day, picking up *The Waves*, *La Nausée*, Vladimir Nabokov's *Pale Fire*, Amos Tutuola's *The Palm-Wine Drinkard*, or *Finnegans Wake*, we may react: 'What do you call this? I don't mind whether I get roast beef (Fielding), or mutton chops, potatoes and batter pudding (Dickens), or oatcakes and black pudding (Bennett), or even salt beef and ship's biscuit (Conrad) or something fried and felicitous; but I can't live on fried grasshoppers, or chocolate-coated ants,[2] or pickled nasturtium seeds, still less on ball-bearings fried in iguana fat! And you might at least put it on a *plate*; I'm not used to eating off the back of a tortoise; besides, it keeps walking away.' This is not a wholly unfair query; we are at liberty not to sample fried grasshoppers; but we must not judge them as beef.

A comprehensive survey of experimental novels would fill a large volume and need a better qualified writer; here I can offer no more than a few hints as to how we may approach novels that are bewilderingly different from mainstream novels.

We should start with a touch of humility, a most vital part of wisdom. If some intelligent people see a novel as valuable and we see it as nonsense, let us first admit the fault may be in our own obtuseness. How many of us can hear a symphony as a composer or conductor hears it? The formula $CH_3CH_2CH_2CH_2OH$ looks to a non-chemist like the first line of a concrete poem about a train crash, but tells a chemist the structure of *n-butyl alcohol* (which leaves the rest of us no wiser). We know whether we can read a musical score, a page of trigonometry, a computer language—Fortran or Algol—or Braille; but, because every day we see pictures and read English, we are less able to realize that some paintings and books demand new kinds of perception. Expecting to understand a novel at first sight, we feel an outraged disappointment before

Finnegans Wake that we would not feel before a page of calculus or Tamil. Sometimes, indeed, we have to admit that we are not at present capable of reading a highly experimental book: we need the help of a textbook, a teacher, or more experience of reading or even of life.

Someone who has never been in love, or had a child, or earned a living, is cut off from full understanding of many novels. A headmaster or general, who has to deal with problems of authority, discipline, dilemmas of collective and individual good, imperfect subordinates, his own weaknesses, professional disloyalty, envy, different people's varying concepts of what a community should be like, will understand *Coriolanus* or Trollope's novels of politics or C. P. Snow's novels of academic life with insights no fifth-former can possibly yet have acquired. We have some notions of truth, courage and loyalty, and of being-in-love, long before we appreciate problems of integrity, the balancing of tolerance with upholding of standards, or the deeper complexities and ambiguities of love. We can relish Scott long before we can make anything of Henry James; we need to have done a great deal of wide reading and probably quite a stint of adult life before we can much appreciate *Ulysses*. We should be ready to believe that we are not mature enough (as readers, or as people) to appreciate something we do not understand. We are always free to say, 'This book is not for me, at least not yet', or even, 'I doubt if this would ever, for me, be worth the time I would have to devote to it', for we have other things to do; but to greet a piece of experimental art with 'This is just a lot of old rubbish!' or 'This is some of that awful modern nonsense!' implies enormous conceit. We are all *ignorant* of the greater part of human knowledge; but to be *arrogant* in ignorance is the temper of wilful barbarism. That the Nazis burned innovatory books and vilified modern art is not a coincidence.

Sometimes people suggest that an experimental work is a

hoax, its maker a charlatan, seeking prestige by being
mysterious. This is possible now and then. Phoney modernism
can be an excuse for not wrestling with technical problems;
this has been known to arise in educational institutions. But
in general common sense refutes the suspicion concerning any
work of any substantial size. If we consider what an effort it is
to write a couple of pages of school composition, what heavy
weather most people make of answering letters, even what a
toil it is just to *copy* something, we see how unlikely it is that a
sane man will write a whole book just as a hoax. *Finnegans
Wake* will never have a mass readership; it is hardly my cup
of Irish coffee either; but once I know that James Joyce worked
on it for seventeen years, struggling against near-blindness
and repeated eye operations, I know he was not a charlatan;
that kind of heroic dedication cannot guarantee a masterpiece,
but it does guarantee sincerity of intention.

Readers can easily pick up an impression that until recently
there was nothing but Good Sound Literature, until there
came a Dreadful Modern Age, in which Things are Falling to
Pieces. I have known even professional teachers, in this respect
mis-educators, imply this view. The one use of such narrowness is that the tutting ugliness, whining spite, gobbling
dogmatism or dismissive shallowness of their contempt
sometimes stimulates in the young, through their equally
arrogant and irrational rebelliousness, a useful intellectual
curiosity and receptivity, in that if Old Turkeyface hates it,
it is probably splendid; but this is a very miserable and
destructive teaching or family situation.

We should bear in mind three facts: that the history of any
art is a series of innovations, with virtually all major works of
art as in some sense experimental in their day, and vilified by
many in their day; that it is impossible to rule a thick black
line between traditional and experimental works; and, in our
present field, that 'eccentric' novels appeared almost as soon
as those we generally regard as typical. In most human

experience there is far more of continuum, overlapping, tangle, and pendulum movement than there is of straight lines and watertight compartments.

Samuel Richardson was an experimenter: fiction on that scale, with that analytic detail, emotional intensity, and level of realism, was new; Walter Scott introduced whole new concepts of the treatment of historical and local background. The Brontës shocked many people in their day almost as much as D. H. Lawrence shocked people in his, by the new candour and intensity with which they treated aspects of passion and feeling. Dickens had not only boiling vitality, but versatile originality. Henry James brought a new approach to the presentation of character and motive and the point-of-view. The greatest art probably does not strain after originality; but it usually includes something notably original.

We find elements we cannot call 'mainstream' in novels we accept as largely 'mainstream': the satire on Richardson in *Joseph Andrews*; the parody of classical epic in *Tom Jones*; the linguistic amusements in *Humphry Clinker*; the satire on the Gothic novel in *Northanger Abbey*; the dream sequences in *Alton Locke*, which include impressionistic sentences with no verbs. Dickens uses symbolism, parody, elements of allegory, invocations, a wealth of small linguistic oddities: we may consider the stylistic inventions used in the tenth chapter of *Little Dorrit* to describe the 'Circumlocution Office', or the moments when Flora becomes startlingly like Molly Bloom! *The Story of an African Farm* contains a noble and moving allegory of the search for truth, told as a stranger's interpretation of the questing but inarticulate Waldo's carving.[3] Eighteenth- and nineteenth-century novelists often put bits of verse into their stories for various purposes.

Many experimental novelists can trace part of their literary ancestry as far back as Lucian, Rabelais, Cervantes,[4] or to works not of prose fiction, such as Greek or Latin epic, Shakespearian drama, philosophical dialogue; but we should also remember that Swift's *Tale of a Tub* appeared in 1704, before *Robinson Crusoe* or *Pamela*; his *Gulliver's Travels* in 1726 and Sterne's *Tristram Shandy* in several volumes from 1759 to 1767; and most subsequent experimental novelists probably owe something to Swift, Sterne or both.

We have had T. L. Peacock's novels of fantasy, satire and personifications of theories; Samuel Butler's thought-provoking *Erewhon* (1872), or the jollier novel of philosophical satire, W. H. Mallock's *The New Paul and Virginia, or Positivism on an Island* (1878) with a dry joke in nearly every sentence. The myth-making, quasi-metaphysical novel, in which much is left unexplained, is Victorian at the latest, as in George Macdonald's *Lilith* (1895) with its illuminations, quests, tasks, redemption myth, riddles and paradoxes. The greatest myth-novelist before this century is probably Herman Melville. Besides *Moby Dick*, he wrote other novels with an enigmatic quality, speaking perhaps in part to the unconscious: *Pierre, or the Ambiguities* is weak as a realistic novel—too 'gothic', and with stilted dialogue—but it is strangely in advance of its time in its insights into ambivalence, symbolic portrayal of unconscious forces, awareness that all moral choices are not as clear as they seem, seeing of all things in 'a dubious, un-certain and refracting light'.

Elements of disintegration and despair are also not new: Melville is disquieting enough, and one of his main ideas is that man cannot 'reconcile the world with his own soul'. There are implications in Swift's fictions to chill anyone. Johnson's short philosophical romance, *Rasselas*, observes that 'Human life is everywhere a state in which much is to be endured, and little to be enjoyed'. Full of shrewd, sad comments on evil and suffering, it is wise and calming rather than cynical. C. R. Maturin's *Melmoth the Wanderer* (1820) has an almost feverish quality of imagination, and, among 'gothic' horrors and awkward structure, some genuine insights into aspects of human malice, suffering, hypocrisy, morbidities in religion, with some corrosive satire and grim ironies. Long before our current post-Hiroshima imaginings of a total collapse of civilization, Mary Shelley in *The Last Man* (1826), at the end of a quasi-philosophical novel with romanticized politics and characters suggestive of Byron and Shelley, has a finale in which Lionel Verney is the last man left alive, with a dog as his last friend, with many pages of vivid and sometimes poetic imaginings.

In the prototypes of much experimental fiction, *A Tale of a Tub* and *Tristram Shandy*, we find little of plot and incident, lifelike character or conversation, or realistic background.

A Tale of a Tub is an allegory, easy to follow once we realize that the brothers, Peter, Martin and Jack, represent respectively the Roman Catholic church, the Church of England, and the Presbyterians and Dissenters. They are left by their father three coats (Christianity) and have to interpret his Will (the New Testament). As Swift was a clergyman in the Church of England, he shows Martin as fairly sensible, while the other two go to ridiculous extremes. We can soon work out many equivalents and enjoy many laughs at the cheeky inventiveness and dotty logic of the satire.

This tale, however, is not a large part of the book. There are lengthy preliminaries, consisting mostly of satires on authors, critics and readers; later there are long Digressions— one about Critics, which also satirizes phoney or pedantic erudition; 'Digression in the Modern Kind' which was partly an attack on William Wotton's now forgotten *Reflections upon Ancient and Modern Learning*, so that the present-day reader misses most of the fun;[5] a Digression in Praise of Digressions; and the one which still has some bite left in it, the 'Digression concerning the Original (*sic*), the Use and Improvement of Madness in a Commonwealth', in which Swift implies that many respectable activities have something of madness in them, and makes some of his disquieting observations on our human condition, such as his definition of Happiness as 'a perpetual Possession of being well Deceived'.

There is no pleasure in reading *A Tale of a Tub* for any of the reasons for which we usually read novels. There is still much pleasure to be had from the wildly cheeky analogies, and such things as the hilarious account of Papal Bulls, with its telling puns and mock-scientific teasing. We may be bored by out-of-date in-jokes, or irritated by some ugly images from Swift's tiresome excremental preoccupation; but we can still see the book as an intellectual romp of genius.

Swift wrote, 'When a true Genius appears in the world, you may know him by this infallible Sign: that the Dunces are all in Confederacy against him.'[6] It is significant that Ray Bradbury, in his dystopian novel *Fahrenheit 451*, portraying a society in which intellectual activity is as far as possible prevented and it is a crime to own a book, chooses *Gulliver's Travels* at one crisis to represent the world of books; for Swift makes us *think*.

There is emotion, some of it sick, behind Swift's inventions, but his stories are mostly intellectual exercises. *Tristram Shandy* has more humanity and warmth. At first sight it looks more like a mainstream novel: there are lifelike characters and some apparently realistic conversation; but we soon find that the time-sequence is dislocated and there is nothing like a normal plot. Though the full title is *The Life and Opinions of Tristram Shandy, Gent.*, we never learn much about Tristram: he is begotten in the first chapter and we have his birth date at the beginning of the fifth; but then we have digressions about hobbies, dedications, a midwife, Parson Yorick's horse and the parson's character and death, Mrs Shandy's marriage settlement, Christian names, baptism, Uncle Toby's character and hobby, bringing us to the end of the twenty-fifth chapter and first volume; and so we go on, with Tristram born in the third volume and baptized in the fourth. He appears occasion- ally again, and grows old enough to be put into breeches, but we never hear much of him as a person, and the novel ends abruptly with a remark about a story of a Cock and a Bull, which seems to sum it up fairly happily. Nor is there a clear, consequential story about anyone else.

How maddening! What, then, has *Tristram Shandy* to offer? A surprisingly up-to-date, brilliant picture of how we often think and talk: led from topic to topic by associations, as when any military allusion leads Uncle Toby, very comically, to his hobby; telling things out of sequence; giving topics relative proportions that are far from rational; displaying knowledge, and so on. There are two real character creations: Mr Walter Shandy, full of 'Shandean notions'— eccentric, dogmatic, dictatorial; and Uncle Toby, with his military hobby and a heart so soft that he (literally) cannot hurt a fly. There is much comic invention in anecdotes and allusions; some breadth of culture, much wit; a great command of surprise, anti-climax and inventive fluency; there is also some rather nudging naughtiness, often witty but eventually becoming a bit overdone. Perhaps the dominant theme is that our personalities need both 'Mr Shandy' and 'Uncle Toby'—thought and feeling—for wise and balanced living.

Sterne was not just rambling; a conscious artist, he often alludes to his odd way of writing a novel; he refers to his digressions as 'the sunshine, the life, the soul of reading' and uses such tricks as:

> My mother, you must know—but I have fifty things more necessary to let you know first:—I have a hundred difficulties which I have promised to clear up, and a thousand distresses and domestic misadventures crowding in upon me thick and threefold, one upon the neck of another.

In Volume VI, Chapter 40, he actually draws five irregular lines as diagrams of how his book is constructed!

In Sterne we find many techniques used in later experimental novels, either well developed, or hinted at in passing.

Off the beaten track

Here are some of these—not arranged in any order of significance.

1 *Dislocations of time*

Unexpected modifications of normal time sequences, or unusual ways of signifying that events occur simultaneously (cf. Virginia Woolf's *The Waves*); or dislocations of ordinary ideas of *proportion*, dwelling at length on matters usually considered trivial, quickly dismissing matters usually considered important.

2 *Allegory*

Cf. Orwell: *Animal Farm*.

3 *Symbolism*

Not sharply definable as allegorical: characters or objects suggest something on a bigger scale, or imply psychological or spiritual concepts in a wider field. Cf. Hemingway: *The Old Man and the Sea*; William Golding: *The Spire*; Iris Murdoch: *The Bell*; J. G. Ballard: *The Crystal World*.

4 *Parody*

Cf. *Ulysses*; and John Barth: *The Sot-Weed Factor*, which is in part a parody of an eighteenth-century novel, with a Journal parodying seventeenth-century English.

5 *Extrapolation*

That is, following some social or other trend, or some idea, to an improbable extreme in order to make a point. Cf. Aldous Huxley: *Brave New World* and *Ape and Essence*; George Orwell: *1984*; and much serious science-fiction.

6 *Typographical and other visual devices*

For example, fancy use of capitals and italics, unusual punctuation, footnotes, marginal notes, tabulation, non-alphabetical peⱥy sıɥ uo ᵷuıpuɐ⊥s

Off the beaten track

notation such as a few bars of music or a drawing; asterisks
and such tricks as may be exemplified by stating that a very
experimental book may make the reader feel he is
·pɐǝɥ sıɥ uo ᵷuıpuɐʇs
Cf. Piglet's sensation of Roo's jumping in *Winnie-the-Pooh*,
and the taily tale of the Mouse in *Alice in Wonderland*. In the
mainstream novel *A Woman-Hater* Charles Reade italicizes the
few true statements in a liar's plausible exposition; Michael
Crichton's *The Andromeda Strain* uses computer-made maps
and diagrams, scientific tables and a graph.

7 Digression

The interpolation of something not at once relevant to any
'story', perhaps in a different style, often with some element
of sheer joy in virtuosity. A *tour de force* is the 'modern
version' of *Oedipus Rex* in John Barth's *Giles Goat-Boy*, using
university terminology, slang and so on.

8 Analogies

Often drastic and startling. In Kafka's *The Trial* life itself is,
by implication, seen as a process of being on trial for an
offence we cannot identify, by procedures we do not understand, with a death sentence at the end; or Bloom's wanderings
during one day in *Ulysses* are seen as an analogy of the
Odyssey.

9 Various semantic experiments

Such as puns, onomatopoeia, portmanteau words, exploita-
tion of ambiguities, word games, puzzles, foreign words,
words and compounds invented by analogy, variants on
parsing ('She fryingpanned him bangly'), nicknames, allusive
names, ironical namings and descriptions, tricks of rhyme,
association, parallelisms, malapropisms and misspellings,
comic long compounds, unusual interjections and so on.
Joyce provides the most spectacular collection of such

ambiguities; Flann O'Brien's *At Swim-Two-Birds* is a lesser example. Semantic amusements in a story for children appear in Norton Juster's delightful *The Phantom Tolbooth*.

10   *Catalogues or lists*

A favourite device of Rabelais and Joyce; some readers find these tedious, others enjoy the exuberance.

11   *Imitations of the methods of scholarship*

Among these we may have spoof footnotes, mention of non-existent books, skits on lecturing techniques. Joyce makes considerable use of this device; Richard Adams in *Watership Down* has charmingly solemn footnotes about rabbit language.

12   *Allusion*

What we sometimes call in-jokes. Cf. Joyce, who demands wide reading and a close knowledge of Dublin. There is lighter use in Caryl Brahms's and S. J. Simon's *No Bed for Bacon*, or Ronald Clark's *Queen Victoria's Bomb*.

13   *Shifts from one mode to another*

Literal to symbolic, realism to fantasy, satire to myth, and so on. Cf. Nathanael West's *Miss Lonelyhearts*, fluctuating between a fairly realistic story and a bitter Christ-myth; Mikhail Bulgakov's *The Master and Margarita*; James Branch Cabell's *Jurgen*. Melville is a master of what looks at first like unsatisfying uncertainty of tone and comes to be seen as conveying multiplicity, ambiguity and the shifting levels and modes of experience in which we live.[7]

14   *Extravagance*

Bursts of exuberance piling on masses of detail, wild invention, comic exaggeration. Rabelais was the great pioneer of this.

15 Profanation

Taking something we expect to see treated seriously, even with awe, and treating it flippantly, satirically or with black humour. Parody often has an element of this. It is not necessarily just negative; it may be thought-provoking or reduce something to reasonable proportions. The dialogues of Lucian, and Byron's *Don Juan*, are examples outside the novel. We find profanation in this sense in Voltaire's *Candide*, in *Turgen*, in Samuel Butler's *The Way of All Flesh* (against the conventional Victorian view of family life); in Jaroslav Hasek's *The Good Soldier Schweik* or Joseph Heller's *Catch-22* (deflating ideas of brave soldiers and noble war-aims); in Evelyn Waugh's *The Loved One* (shocking our natural solemnity about death to show how commercialized sentimentality insults the true seriousness).

16 Sanctification

Giving to things commonplace or despised a new dignity, which affirms a value in life or personality; it may be as shocking in its first impact as 'profanation'.[8] G. K. Chesterton in *Manalive*, using fantasy, surprise, play and paradox to exalt the wonder of everyday objects and relationships; Lawrence in *Lady Chatterley's Lover* and—I think more adequately—Jules Romains in *Psyche* (translated as *The Body's Rapture*), glorifying real sexual relations; John Steinbeck in *Cannery Row* or *Sweet Thursday* bringing out some goodness and grace in disreputable people. I see some in *Ulysses*, with trivial details of a somewhat sordid and commonplace life given a significance commensurate with the infinite possibilities of one human soul; but some readers see only disgust and pessimism.

17 Retelling a known story

With a twist or in an unexpected way. Sterne does this only

on a very small scale. Cf. interpretations of the Gospel story in George Moore's *The Brook Kerith* or Robert Graves's *King Jesus*; of the Arthurian legends in T. H. White's *The Once and Future King*; of the Hamlet story in Henry Treece's *The Green Man* or J. B. Cabell's *Hamlet Had an Uncle*.[9]

18   Unexpected treatment of the 'point of view'

The ambiguities of some of Henry James's creations of character are now common in even mainstream novels. In Conrad's *Lord Jim* the theme would suit an early romance: a man forfeits his honour by an act of cowardice and redeems it by subsequent integrity, unselfishness and courage; but Marlowe, the narrator, repeatedly alludes to a certain ambiguity, and reports Jim as saying, 'There was not the thickness of a sheet of paper between the right and wrong of this affair.' On a superficial level, Dorothy Sayers and Robert Eustace, in *The Documents in the Case*, present the points of view of all concerned in a murder, leaving us with some sense that the complexity of life has at least been acknowledged.

Among devices not used by Sterne at least two should be mentioned.

19   Mixtures of dramatic with narrative presentation

Portions of dialogue are set out as if in a play. A scrap like this may be found in *Robinson Crusoe*. Modern experimental use is more complex, as in *Ulysses*; William Faulkner's *Requiem for a Nun*; Wyndham Lewis's *The Childermass*.

20   Bilingualism

Sterne has several passages using Latin and English, but some modern novelists are bilingual in a different way. There are refugees from Nazi, Communist and sometimes other repressive régimes; there are Africans and Asiatics using English. Numerous Britons are also bilingual, being Welsh or Gaelic speakers.[10] The conflicts and special tensions of such writers must provide new experiences of the nature of language, the imperfections and excitements of communication. An interesting example is Nabokov, notably in *Pnin*, with its expatriate Russian hero thinking in his own brand of English. We may think too of Conrad, George Mikes, Arthur Koestler and Samuel Beckett. (I have myself found that writing books in both English and Esperanto has stimulated such sensitivity to language as I can claim.)

We have heard much lately of the 'anti-hero', the blunderer, sinner, perhaps cynic: Jim Dixon, Wain's Charles Lumley (in *Hurry on Down*, with its delightfully profane Wordsworth quotation as epigraph), perhaps Bellow's Augie March, and Nabokov's Humbert Humbert in *Lolita*. We can no longer accept the Victorian hero; we 'know too much'—psychoanalysis, relativity, economic determinism, behaviourism—and we 'know too little'—we have not yet worked our way through and beyond our disturbing new insights to concepts of goodness and truth that take account of them. This is perhaps the major task for a coming generation of novelists. Some earlier 'anti-heroes' have been mentioned;[11] others include Andy in Samuel Lover's *Handy Andy, a Tale of Irish Life*, and Tittlebat Tittlemouse, nastily selfish as well as vulgar, in Warren's *Ten Thousand a Year*; in greater novels we might also class Goncharov's Oblomov and even Stendhal's Julien Sorel (*Le Rouge et le Noir*) in this category.

A more genuine innovation in technique is the *stream of consciousness* or *interior monologue*, trying to represent more of our mental experience than the small part which is coherent thought: associations, memories, sense impressions, emotion, fantasy, varied levels of consciousness. The inventor of the technique is usually taken to be Dorothy Richardson in her thirteen-volume *Pilgrimage* (1915–38); she told the story partly in traditional narrative and partly in interior monologue. Better known today are Virginia Woolf and James

Joyce. Something of the technique is found in John Dos Passos's *Manhattan Transfer* and still more in his *42nd Parallel*; he also uses, in sections called 'Newsreels', ironically incongruous juxtapositions of headlines and news items, and in sections called 'The Camera Eye' sense-impressions and associations in a more drastically inconsequential train of thought. Dos Passos was concerned mostly with social criticism; J. D. Salinger uses some stream-of-consciousness technique to convey the muddles and anxieties of adolescence; a beginner might well start with Stevie Smith's lighter *Novel on Yellow Paper*. Short bursts of interior monologue are now fairly common in mainstream novels.

Yet even that stream flowed as early as *Tristram Shandy*, where we find inconsequentiality, association of ideas, digression, shifting moods, interruptions, fantasies, parentheses, play, allusion, memories out of chronological sequence, scraps of learning; Sterne gives a picture of the illogicality of mental experience; but he is neither as clinical nor as sensitive as some modern writers, and he represents conversation rather than thought.

The technique creates its own conventions; it cannot be a perfect representation of human consciousness, for which language, typography and the visual range of the reading eye are all inadequate. A great deal of our experience is never verbalized; indeed, for much of it there are no words. (We have a hopelessly small vocabulary even for something as simple as our daily experience of smells and their associations!)

Other experimental methods include the 'non-fiction novel', what may be called the modified-English novel, and the *nouveau roman*.

The 'non-fiction novel', sometimes infelicitously called *faction*, is a kind of high-level compilation. The best-known is Truman Capote's *In Cold Blood*; it can be read as a novel, but is the story of a real murder, written after examination of documents, interviews, and so on. Capote claims that all the material not based on his own observation came from real records or interviews. Something rather like this appeared as early as 1722—Defoe's *Journal of the Plague Year*, based mostly on books and on conversations with people who remembered the Plague of London (1664-6). Defoe quoted real documents, but invented a narrator and modified the facts somewhat. Any sensible novel of social protest, such as *The Grapes of Wrath* or *42nd Parallel* or *Love on the Dole*, will have some documentary sources, though they may not be quoted verbatim.

There are successful African and Commonwealth novelists of marked individuality, and in the coming decades we are likely to see further developments in the modern African novel, with appropriate new literary techniques. The English may not be what we are used to. The Nigerian Amos Tutuola was literate in English but without experience of European culture when he wrote his totally African *The Palm-Wine Drinkard*; its material is African folklore and imagination, its style a kind of Nigerian-English. A man loses his palm-wine tapster and goes to seek him among the Dead—a type of quest as early as the *Epic of Gilgamesh* and the *Aeneid*. On his quest he encounters, among other phenomena, a creature a quarter of a mile long and six feet in diameter, a tree which sprouts hands and has a hospital inside it, a red fish with thirty horns, and four hundred dead babies on a march. Here is a sample:

But as we looked at our back, we were looking at the large hands with fear, so when the hands gave us sign to come to him, now my wife and I betraited ourselves, because the hands told both of us to come to him, my wife pointed me to the hands and I myself pointed her to the hands too; after that my wife forced me to go first and I pushed her to go first. As we were doing that, the hands told us again that both of us were wanted inside the tree, so when we thought that we had never seen a tree with hands and talking in our life, or since we have been travelling in the bushes, then we started to run away as before, but to our surprise, when the hands saw that we took to our heels again, they stretched out from the tree without end and then picked both of us up off the ground as we were running away.

To an English reader such work seems an exotic nightmare, possibly throwing light on 'unknown modes of being'; its impact on a Nigerian is no doubt very different.

This has zest; but the anti-novel, if I understand the theory, is a product of very cerebral, literary, jaded, self-conscious and pessimistic attitudes. Its chief practitioners are French: Claude Simon, Michel Butor, Alain Robbe-Grillet and Nathalie Sarraute; Christine Brooke-Rose has sometimes been thought of as kin to them, and some would add Samuel Beckett, whose *Malone meurt* is written with marvellous exactness—and beside it Hardy's novels appear to brim over with hope and joy.[12]

Robbe-Grillet is perhaps the most uncompromising of the writers of the *nouveau roman*, who insist on a total separation of Man from the natural world, avoiding even the hint of relationship in an expression like 'the cruel cold'. Their novels give an impression of extreme impersonality, the chaos and flux of life, the discontinuity of experience, and how we desire order but never achieve it. They distort our everyday ideas of relative importance, by dwelling on minor details in preference to critical events. For instance, in Robbe-Grillet's *Le Voyeur* there is a murder, but we are left with a sense of the unimportance of life and death, character or motive, while wonderful care goes to describing the water at the side of a ship or liquid being poured from a bottle. In his *La Jalousie* there is a love affair, but our attention is claimed mostly for such things as the arrangement of banana trees, the mechanics of eating, or the squashing of a centipede. (Possibly several; the overlappings and dislocations of time sequence are such that I confess I was not sure how many centipedes were squashed.) Minute details of furniture in Nathalie Sarraute's *Le Planétarium* have rather more obvious human relevance, in that furniture can be important to ordinary people; and this novel includes rather more recognizable human emotions, with some use of a kind of stream of consciousness. Michael Butor's *Degrés*, gives equal importance to a lesson, a dangerous illness, a divorce, or a man's wish to write something truthful, and has some humour in the contrasts of lessons on great topics of human history or culture with the irrelevant behaviour of most of the boys—occupied with fantasies, doodling or stamp collecting—or in its contrast of the school study of Rabelais, expurgated, and what is possible in a French *lycée*, with Rabelais's grand-scale views on education.

I believe these novelists, influenced by aspects of modern philosophy and psychology, wish to write a new kind of novel emphasizing discontinuity, uncertainty, the inadequacy or language as being too logical and orderly to represent experience, and the actual process of composition. The anti-novels I have seen strike me as full of brilliant sentences and studied artistry, original, intelligent and ultimately arid, even dull. Younger readers may well achieve a more positive response.

Christine Brooke-Rose, translator of some of Robbe-Grillet, seems to me a novelist of more humanity and scope. Her *Out* has Swiftian elements of satire on racism, with conversations, in an apocalyptic post-nuclear-catastrophe framework, that are mirror images of today's unreasonings; she uses medical terminologies, some realistic, some fantastic, to suggest some of our horrors and fears. She has great linguistic ingenuity (for example, the end of white dominance is implied by turning 'American' and 'British' into 'Uessayan' and 'Ukayan'), and a good deal of angry compassion. Her *Between* may be seen as an anti-novel in that it is largely about human efforts to communicate and failures of communication; it tells the story of a woman's divorce and unhappy love-life obliquely (or more straight than we can take?) without the usual narrative or explanatory intermediaries. It has an almost Joycean linguistic inventiveness, such as its use of sentences, often partly clichés, that switch construction and content midway with startling effect. As, on top of experimental techniques, Miss Brooke-Rose shows considerable erudition, her work makes heavy demands on the reader; but it has more vitality than the French works mentioned above, and offers worthwhile rewards.

Another kind of anti-novel is that of William Burroughs, with his *fold-in* technique, which I believe he regards as an 'exploded novel': the repetition of images and various over-lappings give a sense that time itself has slipped into chaos. Elements of science-fiction, social and political satire, nightmare, travel book, spy story, philosophical discourse and so on are interwoven in rapidly changing modes, and in *The Ticket that Exploded* one idea is that communication must be made 'total' by grotesque, extrapolated use of tape-recorders and splicings of tape and film, in order that—communication may come to an end.

A novel can be highly experimental without abandoning traditional narration, time sequence and sentence structure. For instance, John Barth's *Giles Goat-Boy* is almost a direct descendant of *A Tale of a Tub*. Intellectually stimulating and quite demanding, it does not ask the reader for a wholly new approach. It allegorizes the world as a vast American-style university run, ultimately, by giant computers. Several religions, political persuasions, aspects of philosophy, history or culture are reduced to absurdity—or brought into new focus for rethinking—by being described in terms of academic administration. The hero is a messiah or pseudo-messiah begotten by a computer; the book raises several questions of theology and psychology, but (as I read it) leaves them unanswered. With satire, wit and outrageous cheek we do find some compassion and some small respect towards human beings for trying so hard. Such an experimental novel is likely to be more enjoyable for most readers than one that abandons the whole familiar structure of fiction or even of language.

Ulysses and *Finnegans Wake* probably remain today the supreme examples of the spectacularly experimental novel, and must have played a major part in expanding our ideas on the novel and on language. There have been two wildly misleading ways of reading them. One is to hunt in them for smut, as children at the prurient stage sometimes hunt in the Bible. Joyce and the Bible are both concerned with life, which includes sex and excretion; enlightenment and love are the chief cleansing agents for what unhappy or ignorant people see as dirty; laughter too can cleanse and heal. To see Joyce (or Lawrence) as smutty implies, in my view, a mind either immaturely prurient, or neurotically puritanical. The other wrong approach is to pick a paragraph or two that is not at once understandable, and on such evidence reject the whole thing as a lot of modern nonsense. It does take us a long time to come to terms with sex—really quite difficult in a complex civilization—but at least let us avoid being great lumps of ignorant arrogance! When Joyce asked for readers who would spend a lifetime on his work, he asked too much— even specialists in literature have other things to do. But, though free to decide we have no time to read something, we have no right to dismiss a dedicated man's life-work in a few minutes and claim our opinion has any value.

These two novels, however, are for experienced and fairly mature readers, who will still probably need help. We need wide reading, including reading much closer than just follow-ing a story; wide general knowledge; educated awareness of language and some knowledge of foreign languages; and a fair range of adult experience. The last does not refer to those aspects that once caused *Ulysses* to be banned: most teenagers know something of both the splendours and the miseries of sexuality, and all know the messy ignominies of our bodily nature. What only further experience can give is the layered sense of the past; the understanding of the motives of Bloom's concern for Stephen; his and Molly's rueful tolerance of each other; individuals felt in relation to geography, history, and mankind; or a real sense of mutability and mortality. And unless our own education has progressed a fair distance, we cannot relish the wonderful ironies and pathos of Bloom's half-education and cultural muddle.

Ulysses is a major, moving novel; its power and compassion can grow on the reader. To appreciate it fully one needs a detailed knowledge of Joyce's biography; of the Dublin he knew; of Irish history, mythology, folklore, song, geography, literature; of English and world literature; of the classical background to European culture; of Catholic theology, education, liturgy; of the sub-literature of the period—trashy magazines, advertisements, etc.; of music and philosophy, non-Catholic religions and superstitions; etymology and languages; *plus* the ability to sort out the story, situations and characters presented obliquely. However, without full appreciation a reader can find some real pathos and much sheer fun. For instance, the birth of a child, with invocations and meditations, is described in a series of very funny parodies from literature in chronological order—amusing even if we do not realize that the history of literature is being used to symbolize our development before birth. There are skits on Victorian moralizing novelettes, on bad journalism, on academic examinations and other special uses of language. We also find in *Ulysses*, as in *Tristram Shandy* but on a bigger scale, an anthology of the techniques of experimental fiction.

Finnegans Wake is another matter. *Ulysses* is an extreme and marvellous demonstration of the possibilities of the English language; *Finnegans Wake* is not written in English, in any usual sense, and readers who can fully read it must be very rare. (I am not among them.) It is written in an English-based mixture of most of the modern European languages, plus Latin, Greek, Sanskrit, Esperanto (modified but recognizable) and several other tongues, with a wealth of puns, double meanings, multiple meanings, onomatopoeia and staggeringly complex structures of cultural allusions. The sheer *layeredness* of the work adds to the difficulty. There are some characters: the dying Finnegan; the 'Everyman' figure, H. C. Earwicker; his wife Anna Livia Plurabelle; their sons Shem and Shaun and their daughter, with identifiable minor characters. But everyone stands for several images, concepts, persons—for example, Anna is also the River Liffey. No ordinary reader is likely to appreciate *Finnegans Wake* without holding the hand of a specialist scholar through the whole weird and wonderful journey.[13] The reader who would like to sample it but has little time might try the character study of Shem the Penman, disreputable creative artist, partly a self-portrait of Joyce, in the seventh section of Book I[14] and the beautiful last pages in which the river Liffey flows into the sea.

Such sampling would give a fair idea of how Joyce was using language, but not of the vast scope of the book, which is an attempt at a language expressive of total world civilization and the totality of human experience.[15] It was written under the influence of the Italian philosophers Vico and Bruno, whom few of us have studied.[16] When we have some inkling of what it is about, it can be very moving as well as funny; yet the fact that even educated readers need specialist help shows how restricted is the communication. Today Shakespeare needs a few footnotes; refuse to fetch a chair to pick delicious apples, and you deserve to go hungry. *Finnegans Wake* asks us to climb a thousand-foot tree to pick fruit we may not like. The fruit at the top is a crystal ball with a world inside it, but it is a very hard way up; an extreme of experimental literature.

Yet all can dip and savour at least some fun: soup swallowed 'swp by swp', a baby squalling in its 'crydle'; anyone who has held authority knows what it means to be 'ultimendly respunchable', and most of us have been 'eleven thirsty' or gone through a week of 'moanday, tearsday, wailsday, thumpsday, frightday, shatterday'; the miseries caused by religious fanaticism are summed up neatly in 'howly rowsary' and 'envenomoloped in piggotry'; and most people can sometimes protest that, 'I've a terrible errible lot todue todie todue tootorrible day!'

We should also read a few passages aloud, as the rhythms are often so beautiful that bits of the book can be enjoyed as word-music without much understanding. I believe a thorough study of *Finnegans Wake* would be a tremendous intellectual experience; it might well be a major spiritual experience; but most of us do have a hurrybell tirable lot todue tootrue and cannot mark the joyce!

Experiments break new ground and the great main stream flows on. We hear talk of the impending 'death of the novel'. We could destroy all life worth living, with privacy and leisure for the arts and affections—by overpopulation, nuclear or biological war, totalitarianism, ecological irresponsibility; but great literature does help a little towards that very responsibility, tolerance, foresight, compassion, maturity we need. If humanity solves its pressing problems (as it generally does), new media offer alternatives to reading; but the novel has still much to give. Rapid developments in science, technology, social organization, ideas on human relationships, experiences of scale and perspective, give the novelist abundant new material; in spite of distresses and perplexities, frontiers of experience and consciousness do move outwards; some day we could even have enough leisure to think about them adequately. People are inexhaustibly varied and interesting; there seems to be no reason why we should lose interest in ourselves. And if no more novels were written, the old ones would still tell us things worth knowing, even if they increasingly required some historical imagination. (Historical imagination is anyway a most valuable mental accomplishment; besides enriching life, it helps to reduce the anxieties and heartaches caused by the generation gap.)

Let us hope, then, that the novel has a long future before it. It provides a recreation that needs little space or equipment, makes no noise or mess and interferes with no one else's comfort. It is the literary form that now appeals to the largest public. Above all, it can widen our sympathies, sensitize our perceptions, train us in details of charity and tolerance, sharpen our intellects, educate our imaginations and even enrich and deepen our emotions; and these, not gadgets or fashions, status or speed, greedy getting or show-off spending, are the true measures of civilization.

NOTES

Chapter 1   The concept of fiction

1 See F. J. Nicholson, *Quakers and the Arts*, Friends Home Service Committee, 1968.
2 *Father and Son*, 1907.
3 Letter to Miss C. M. Symons, 2 January 1888.
4 *The Anatomy of Criticism*, Princeton, 1957.

Chapter 2   Verisimilitude

1 The novel appeared in 1905; the translation by Katsue Shibata and Motonari Kai appeared in Tokyo in 1961.
2 *She*, Chapter 1.
3 'A Case of Identity', from *The Adventures of Sherlock Holmes*, 1861.
4 *Lovers' Vows*, adapted from the German of August von Kotzebue by Mrs Inchbald, 1768. Mrs Inchbald says in an introduction that she had made Amelia, the heroine, declare her love in 'whimsical insinuations' as opposed to the 'coarse abruptness' of the original. She worked from a literal translation of the German, a language she did not know. It is arguable that some of the objection to *Lovers' Vows* is that rehearsing the mild love scenes was not wise for the people involved, by reason of their own emotional uncertainties. But today we might say that a love so easily diverted was not worth much; and Jane Austen seems to expect us to see the play as anyway very unsuitable for private theatricals.

Chapter 3   The point of view

1 For example, Virginia Woolf's *Orlando* is said to have been in part a study of a friend, and Simone de Beauvoir's *The Mandarins* includes recognizable portraits of French intellectuals; there must in such novels be allusions that reinforce the interest for a minority in the know, but that the general public misses.
2 Preface to *The Golden Bowl*, 1909 edition.

Notes

Chapter 5   Character

1 The terms I have used here are not accepted critical technical terms in this context, and should not be used in academic essays or examinations without explanation.

Chapter 6   How character is revealed

1 Patrick Hamilton intended to write a series of novels leading to the execution of Gorse, but did not complete the project.

2 *Quasi*-psychoanalytical, because genuine psychoanalysis is a difficult and time-consuming therapeutic technique; novelists merely borrow some of the insights which the works of psycho-analysts suggest to the intelligent layman. Quasi-psychoanalytical discussion, whether in fiction or in real life, can improve our self-knowledge, understanding of others, and so our charity; but we should remember that even the disciplined and exacting real technique is by no means infallible, and that when watered-down psychoanalytical theories, inevitably amateurish at best, become a technique for sneering, dismissiveness or mere knowingness, they are a way of becoming not more, but less wise and perceptive.

3 'Victoria Lucas' was the pen-name of the poet Sylvia Plath.

Chapter 7   Conversation

1 The nearest we shall get is perhaps Boswell's *Life of Samuel Johnson* and other books purporting to record the talk of some famous man; but even if these are accurate, the words of a distinguished writer on serious topics do not tell us much about ordinary people's everyday talk. One odd source of information is Swift's *A Complete Collection of Genteel and Ingenious Conversation* (often known as *Polite Conversation*); this sounds horribly like some of the vapid, cliché-ridden conversation we hear, but Swift would, as a satirist, be exaggerating to make his point.

2 Conrad's original name was Teodor Jozef Konrad Nałecz Korzeniowski. His second language was French and he learned English only in his twenties, yet became a major English novelist. To the end of his days he spoke English with a strong accent, and may indeed not have had an ear to perceive foreign accents in English well enough to represent them.

Notes

Chapter 8 Scene and background

1 In *You Only Live Twice* there is so much (highly sensational and selective) Japanese background that a Shakespeare-steeped reader complained that here was but one half-pennyworth of Bond to an intolerable deal of *sake*.

2 Italo Svevo's *Senilità*, translated by Beryl de Zoëte as *As a Man Grows Older*, does not deal with old age in any usual sense; the hero is thirty-five. One of the few comforting observations on old age I have ever met in a novel is from Mrs Gaskell's *Mary Barton*:

> 'Yo're mourning for me, my dear? and there's no need, Mary. I'm as happy as a child. I sometimes think I am a child, whom the Lord is hushabying to my long sleep. For when I were a nurse-girl, my missis always telled me to speak very soft and low, and to darken the room that her little one might go to sleep; and now all noises are hushed and still to me, and the bonny earth seems dim and dark, and I know it's my Father lulling me away to my long sleep. I'm very well content; and yo mustn't fret for me.'

3 Let me make it clear that, while to wear blinkers is foolish, to force them on to other people is far worse. This is one reason why censorship, however well intentioned, is so dangerous to intellectual and moral development.

Chapter 10 Off the beaten track

1 *The Pooh Perplex* is a splendid skit on various schools of criticism; besides being great fun, it is a warning against narrow theories and a too close discipleship; it shows how we all tend to read our own preoccupations into any work of art. 'Professor Sweat' represents the slovenly popularizer, too eager to be popular.

2 Fried grasshoppers and chocolate coated ants are edible; I have tasted them, though with more curiosity than enthusiasm. Fried grasshoppers taste rather like liquorice-flavoured potato crisps.

3 The same novel contains, as part of the portrait of the wicked and despicable Bonaparte Blenkins, a neat and bitter definition of his attitude and that of all his tribe, all enemies of growth:

> 'Whenever you come into contact with any book, person, or

Notes

opinion of which you absolutely comprehend nothing, declare that book, person or opinion to be immoral. Bespatter it, vituperate against it, strongly insist that any man or woman harbouring it is a fool or a knave, or both. Carefully abstain from studying it. Do all that in you lies to annihilate that book, person, or opinion.'

4 All now available in readable modern translations in the Penguin series.

5 In fact Swift's satire on Wotton, a gifted man unlucky enough to be opposed by a genius, is neither very funny nor very fair. Wotton's book contains some good sense, wide knowledge, and a tolerably lucid style. He was not just an ass; and Swift could have learned something of tolerance from him.

6 *Thoughts on Various Subjects.*

7 One of the best novels yet written in Esperanto is of this rare type: Julio Baghy's *Hura!* (1930)—an unexpected sophistication in a literature which began only in 1887.

8 The examination-bent reader should be warned that many of my terms in this list are not generally recognized and should not be used without explanation.

9 The Hamlet theme reappears in John Wain's *Feng* poems.

10 The Manx language survives and attempts are being made to revive Kernewek (Cornish), so other British bilingualisms could appear.

11 See pp. 80-1.

12 Beckett is a philosophical (or perhaps anti-philosophical) novelist, much influenced by Bergson and Schopenhauer; but I have neither the space nor the competence to enlarge on this.

13 *A Skeleton Key to Finnegans Wake*, by Joseph Campbell and Henry Morton Robinson, is very helpful; the interpretations are not infallible, but are based on much knowledge and intelligence.

14 Faber edition, pp. 169-95.

15 Hugh MacDiarmid has a similar preoccupation: see his *In Memoriam James Joyce*, 1955.

16 Giovanni Battista Vico (1668-1744) led, rather like Joyce, a dedicated life of study and writing under severe difficulties. He held that 'this world of nations is the work of man, and its explanation therefore only to be found in the mind of man', and

he brought his theories of psychology and history to his account of the development of civilizations. He saw all history as moving in cycles: primitive aristocracy—democracy—empire—barbarism. The thunderclaps, represented by lines of onomatopoeia in Joyce, are taken from Vico's theory of history.

Giordano Bruno (*c.* 1548–1600) was in his own day a heroically advanced independent thinker, who was imprisoned by the Inquisition and died at the stake. His allegorical mode of thinking, philosophical quest for unity, and belief that the highest function of the soul was to contemplate the divine unity, which he saw in the many-sided universe, appealed to Joyce.

In technique Joyce owes something to both Swift and Sterne; and Swift appears in *Finnegans Wake* often enough to be almost one of its minor myths.

SUGGESTIONS FOR
FURTHER READING

The student of literature who wants to appreciate the art of the novelist more intelligently and zestfully may be helped by further reading of criticism. This list is chosen with a view to its usefulness to the person who has just finished this book. There are numerous other studies of the novel, of particular kinds of novel, and of individual novelists; many not listed here are very good.

Yet the reading of *critical works* is not a substitute for reading *novels*. Critics or teachers or librarians will not all agree on selection or order of merit, but an enquiring reader can easily sort out a sensible list of novels widely believed to be of something like the first rank. A substantial and varied selection of such novels, read with thoughtful attention, will give the reader experience and awareness no critic can give, and equip him to read critics knowing what they are talking about, without which they can do us more harm than good.

Some fairly easy studies

Walter Allen, *Reading a Novel*. Phoenix House, London, 1949. Thirty-three pages of common sense for the beginner, with eight short essays on twentieth-century novelists.

Anthony Burgess, *The Novel Now. A student guide to contemporary fiction*. Faber, London, 1967. A helpful handbook for the general reader; stylishly written, as one might expect from a serious novelist; covers more than Anglo–American literature. No one will agree with every single judgment, but no one will fail to learn something.

E. M. Forster, *Aspects of the Novel*. Edward Arnold, London, 1927. A small classic, helpfully thought-provoking.

Caroline Gordon, *How to Read a Novel*. Viking Press, New York,

Suggestions for further reading

1953. A short, thought-provoking introduction, very readable and making many useful points.

H. W. Leggett, *The Idea in Fiction*. Allen & Unwin, London, 1934. Not, as might be supposed, about didactic fiction, but on aspects of plot and the treatment of it; a small sensible book that would help most readers.

Robert Liddell, *Some Principles of Fiction*. Jonathan Cape, London, 1953. A short study that makes some useful points, though its negative attitudes to the present century are a little overdone and become irritating.

Percy Lubbock, *The Craft of Fiction*. Jonathan Cape, London, 1921. A sensible, modest small book, treating mostly of the 'point of view'.

Edwin Muir, *The Structure of the Novel*. Hogarth Press, London, 1928. A lucid, sensible book making some good points, particularly on the treatment of time, as might be expected from a good poet much concerned with time.

Dorothy Van Ghent, *The English Novel: Form and Function*. Harper, New York, 1953. Intended for the general reader; illustrates her ideas by essays on a number of major novels.

Historical

Walter Allen, *The English Novel*. Phoenix House, London, 1954. One of the more useful histories of the novel for the general reader; one need not agree with every verdict to find much common sense and many useful points.

Arnold Kettle, *An Introduction to the English Novel*. Hutchinson, London, 1951. A short history with some examples treated in more detail. Invites us to think; a strong and perhaps excessive emphasis on questions of class and society.

A few more advanced studies

Wayne C. Booth, *The Rhetoric of Fiction*. Chicago University Press, 1961. Scholarly, full of detailed references, urbanely written and very readable, but hard going for the beginner.

Suggestions for further reading

Q. D. Leavis, *Fiction and the Reading Public*. Chatto & Windus, London, 1932. Should be read both as a possible corrective to my slighter book, and because it is thought-provoking. Mrs Leavis takes a sternly fastidious attitude to fiction, wholly deploring the fantasy and relaxation aspect. She presents interesting quotations and makes important points, but in her concern for discrimination may be too ready to despise.

Simon O. Lesser, *Fiction and the Unconscious*. Beacon Press, Boston, 1957. There has been much jargon-ridden or arrogantly knowing criticism based on psychoanalytical theory, but this is a fine book with broad humanity, proportion, style and sensitivity, illuminating and somewhat original without extravagance.

A. A. Mendilow, *Time and the Novel*. Peter Nevill, London, 1952. Hard, but worth reading. Assumes a good knowledge of the novel.

Philip Stevick (editor), *The Theory of the Novel*. Free Press, New York; Collier-Macmillan, London, 1967. A valuable anthology of studies on the subject, including Northrop Frye's 'The Four Forms of Fiction' and Norman Friedman's 'Forms of the Plot'.

Lionel Trilling, *The Liberal Imagination*. Macmillan, London, 1940. This deservedly famous volume includes three fine essays relevant to the novel: 'Manners, Morals and the Novel', 'Art and Fortune', and 'The Meaning of a Literary Idea'.

INDEX

Index

Index

Index

Index

Index

Index

Index

Index

Index

Index